AWAKENING GIANTS,
FEET OF CLAY

AWAKENING GIANTS,
FEET OF CLAY

ASSESSING THE ECONOMIC
RISE OF CHINA AND INDIA

PRANAB BARDHAN

PRINCETON UNIVERSITY PRESS   PRINCETON AND OXFORD

Library of Congress Cataloging-in-Publication Data
Bardhan, Pranab K.
Awakening giants, feet of clay : assessing the economic rise of China and India /
Pranab Bardhan.
p. cm.

Includes bibliographical references and index.
ISBN 978-0–691–12994–5 (hardback : alk. paper) 1. China—Economic policy—
2000– 2. India—Economic policy—1991– 3. China—Economic
conditions—2000– 4. India—Economic conditions—1991– 5. China—Social
conditions—2000– 6. India—Social conditions—20th century. I. Title.
HC427.95B37 2010
330.951—dc22   2009034252

British Library Cataloging-in-Publication Data is available
This book has been composed in Goudy Oldstyle
Printed on acid-free paper. ∞
press.princeton.edu

Printed in the United States of America

1 3 5 7 9 10 8 6 4 2

CONTENTS

PREFACE

This is a short book on two large countries, focusing on their comparative economic development in the past quarter century (a minuscule segment of their long history). It is not about their now considerable impact on the global economy, which gets most of the attention in the Western media; it is more about what has happened to the lives of people inside those countries and under what structural constraints. Nor is it about the impact of the current global recession; the deliberate focus in the book is on long-term institutional and political-economic issues. It does not represent new frontiers of research; it largely draws on existing information and scholarship. Avoiding the minutiae of analytical or empirical details, it tries with broad-brush strokes to portray the overall contours in a relatively coherent exercise in comparative political economy meant for a general readership. In the process it also demolishes some of the myths popular in the media and parts of academia that have accumulated around the significant economic achievements of the two countries.

Thanks (nonincriminating) are due to Tarun Khanna, Gérard Roland, and two referees for valuable comments on an earlier draft.

Pranab Bardhan
Berkeley, April 2009

AWAKENING GIANTS,
FEET OF CLAY

Chapter 1

Introduction: The Myths Floating around the Giants

> . . . and I know too much now
> To really feel at home in any one place
> —from the Malaya-born poet Goh Poh Seng's
> *As Though the Gods Love Us*

O ver the past few years the media, particularly the financial press, have been all agog over the rise of China and India in the international economy (and how they have done relatively well even in the current global downturn). After a long period of relative stagnation, these two countries, containing nearly two·fifths of the world population, have had their incomes growing at remarkably high rates over the past quarter century or so. In 1820 these two countries contributed nearly half of world income; in 1950 their share was less than one·tenth; currently it is about one-fifth, and the projection is that in 2025 it will be about one-third.[1]

India was slightly ahead of China in 1870 as well as in the 1970s in terms of the level of per capita income at international prices, but since then, particularly since 1990, China has surged well ahead of India. India's per capita income growth rate in the past two decades has been nearly 4 percent. China's has been at least double

---

[1] These share estimates are by Maddison (2007). His income estimates are all at 1990 international prices. These estimates may be somewhat revised once the new World Bank purchasing power parity numbers are used.

that rate, and even discounting for some overstatement in the Chinese official rates of growth, China has clearly grown significantly faster than India. In the world trade of manufacturing, China, and in that of services, India, have made big strides, much to the (as yet largely unfounded) consternation of workers and professionals in rich countries. Apart from attracting substantial foreign investment to their own large domestic markets, global companies originating from these two countries have started flexing their muscles in acquiring companies in Western markets. Journalists have referred to the economic reforms and integration of these large countries into the world economy in all kinds of colorful metaphors: giants shaking off their "socialist slumber," "caged tigers" unshackled, and so on. Newspaper columnists and media pundits have sent breathless reports from Beijing and Bangalore about the imminent and inexorable competition from these two new whiz kids in a hitherto complacent neighborhood in a "flattened," globalized playing field. Others have warned about the momentous implications of "three billion new capitalists," largely from China and India, redefining the next phase of globalization.[2]

Although I believe there is some exaggeration in this buildup and in the supposed difficulty of the rich countries in coping, this book is *not* a reexamination of the challenges that China and India pose for the rest of the world either in economic or geopolitical terms. It is more an attempt to look inside these two countries and carry out a comparative assessment of their economic achievements and their still massive problems, with the focus on structural and institutional issues in the domestic political-economy context. My purpose is also less to draw policy lessons than to understand what has happened and under what structural constraints. In the subsequent pages there will be less emphasis on short-run macroeconomic issues (such as those relating to the immediate global financial crisis, or to monetary or exchange rate matters, or to business cycles or panicky withdrawals of international portfolio investment or the trade credit crunch or stimulus packages

[2] See, for example, Friedman (2005), Prestowitz (2005).

or adjustments to sudden shocks, internal or external, which are the staples of daily business news), and more on long-term trends and problems. For these two countries with a long history, however, I'll concentrate largely on what happened in the past quarter century.

In this short book we cannot go into much depth on any question, obviously, but we'll try to be on guard against the hype and oversimplifications that afflict many recent accounts of the two economies. One such oversimplification relates to the issue of democracy or authoritarianism either facilitating or hindering development. We shall discuss some of the complexities of this issue in relation to China and India in our concluding chapter. Another relates to the preoccupation with income growth rates; apart from noting some problems with the growth rate estimates, we'll try to go beyond national average income growth and delve a bit deeper into the anatomy of the political-economic forces, particularly those relating to distributive conflicts. In both countries such conflicts are often rankling and simmering just below the surface. When in recent years I read many of the glowing accounts of the two economies, laid out in rather simplistic and aggregative terms, I was reminded of what Henry James wrote in a different context (in his 1909 preface to *The Princess Casamassima*) about "our not knowing . . . and trying to ignore what 'goes on' irreconcilably, subversively, beneath the vast smug surface."

Many years ago when I was teaching at the Delhi School of Economics, I was once asked by my friend and colleague the late Dharma Kumar, if I had freedom of choice to live in India or China, which would I choose, ignoring the obvious cultural constraints (such as my not knowing the Chinese language). I think I disappointed her when I said that if I were poor, I'd probably choose living in China. Today I am less sure of my answer, even though the Chinese poor are materially even better off now compared to the Indian poor than when I was asked that question. Today I sometimes feel that my (somewhat evasive) answer may be on the lines of the quotation from the Goh Poh Seng poem cited in the epigraph to this chapter.

II

For about one hundred years before Liberation in 1949 in China, and for about two hundred years before Independence in 1947 in India, the encounter of these two countries with the international powers has not been altogether pleasant. There are disputes among historians about how much of the economic stagnation and relative decline in this period is due to that encounter. But there is no dispute today that the rise of China and India, and the (partial) restoration of their earlier important place in the world economy within a rather short span of time (a little more than a quarter century) has been one of the most striking phenomena in recent history in the international economy. To explain this phenomenon, it has been common to use a set of simple generalizations that seem to have now become part of the conventional wisdom. The familiar story runs along the lines of the following two paragraphs.

Many decades of socialist controls and regulations stifled enterprise in both countries and led them to a dead end. Their recent market reforms and global integration have finally unleashed their entrepreneurial energies. Their energetic participation in globalized capitalism has brought about high economic growth in both countries, which in turn led to a large decline in their massive poverty. The two countries are now full of billions of "new capitalists" striving to find their place in the sun. Although India's performance in this respect has been substantial, it has been overshadowed by the really dramatic performance of China both in economic growth and poverty reduction. China has now become the manufacturing "workshop of the world." China's explosive industrial growth in the past quarter century is hailed as historically unique, even better than the earlier East Asian "miracles." Like those "miracles," China's is often regarded as another successful story of a "developmental state," with an active industrial policy and a state-financed and -guided program of industrialization.

China's better performance than India's suggests that authoritarianism may be more conducive to development at early stages, as we have seen earlier in South Korea, Taiwan, and Singapore. In the Chinese case, however, regional economic decentralization provided some dispersal of power and more autonomy and incentives to local people, and even with-

out democracy it led to broad-based local development (unlike in Russia, where regional decentralization led to collusion between local governments and oligarchs, only recently curbed by a semiauthoritarian and centralized Putin administration). Global capitalism, however, has inevitably brought rising inequalities, more in China than in India, and this may portend some problems for the future political stability in China, as it does not have the capability of democratic India to let off the steam of inequality-induced discontent. But all is not lost for democracy in China. The prospering middle classes will, slowly but surely, demand more democratic rights and usher in democratic progress in China, as they have in South Korea and Taiwan.

There are, of course, elements of truth in this story, but through constant repetition it has acquired a certain authoritativeness that, closer scrutiny shows, it does not deserve. Much of this book will challenge different parts of this oversimplified story.

First, two relatively small points about industrial growth in China. While China is possibly the largest single manufacturing production center in the world in many goods in terms of volume, it is not so in terms of value added. Contrary to the popular impression, the world share of manufacturing value added in Japan or the United States is still substantially higher (more than double) than in China. Similarly, although the industrial growth rate has been phenomenal in China, it is not historically unique. Figure 1 in our next chapter shows the growth in value added in the secondary sector (manufacturing, mining, utilities, and construction) during the *first quarter century* of accelerated growth, in China (from 1978), along with comparable figures for three other East Asian countries during their growth spurts: Japan (from 1955), Taiwan (from 1960), and South Korea (from 1965). China outpaces Japan in this period, but not the other two countries. Of course, China's scale makes the growth event huge and incomparable to the growth of the other three countries.

More important, consider the oft-repeated point that it was global integration that brought about high income growth, which then brought down the extreme poverty that had afflicted China and India over many decades or even centuries. First, contrary to popular impression, China's growth has not been primarily export-driven.

As we'll suggest in the next chapter, in terms of growth accounting, the impact of net exports on China's growth in the period 1990–2005 has been relatively modest compared to the impact of domestic investment or consumption. Second, China had major strides in foreign trade and investment mainly in the 1990s and particularly in the subsequent decade; yet already between 1978 and 1993, before those strides, China had a very high average annual growth rate of about 9 percent. As we'll show in chapters 2 and 7, much of the high growth in the first half of the 1980s and the associated dramatic decline in poverty happened largely because of internal factors, not globalization. These internal factors include an institutional change in the organization of agriculture, the sector where poverty was largely concentrated, and an egalitarian distribution of land-cultivation rights, which provided a floor on rural income-earning opportunities, and hence helped to alleviate poverty. Even in the period since the mid-1980s there is a great deal of evidence that domestic public investment in education, agricultural research and development, and rural infrastructure has been a dominant factor in rural poverty-reduction in China.

While expansion of exports of labor-intensive manufactures may have lifted many people out of poverty in China in the past decade or so, the same is not true for India, where exports are still mainly skill- and capital-intensive. It is also not completely clear that economic reform is mainly responsible for the recent high growth rate in India. Reform has clearly made the Indian corporate sector more vibrant and competitive, but most of the Indian economy is not in the corporate sector, with 94 percent of the labor force working outside this sector, public or private. Consider the fast-growing service sector, where India's information technology–enabled services have made a reputation the world over while employing less than one-half of 1 percent of the total Indian labor force. Service subsectors such as finance, business services (including those IT-enabled services), and telecommunications, where reform may have made a significant difference, constitute only about a quarter of the total service-sector output. Two-thirds of this service output is in traditional or "unorganized" activities, in tiny enterprises often below the policy radar, unlikely to have been directly affected, to any substantial extent, by the regulatory or foreign trade policy reforms. It is yet to be empirically and convincingly demonstrated how the small corporate sector benefiting from reforms pulled up the vast informal sector.

As for poverty in India, the national household survey data suggest that the rate of decline in poverty has not accelerated in 1993–2005, the period of intensive opening of the economy, compared to the 1970s and 1980s, and that some nonincome indicators of poverty such as those relating to child health, already rather dismal, have hardly improved in recent years. The growth rate in the agricultural sector, where most of the poor are, has declined somewhat in the past decade, largely on account of the decline of public investment in rural infrastructure, which has little to do with globalization. Also, those who envisage "billions of new capitalists" in China and India do not realize that hundreds of millions of poor people in both countries are currently scrounging a living from tiny family enterprises of extremely low productivity, and they don't have the kind of access to credit, marketing, and infrastructure or the basic skills and education and risk-bearing capacity that can make a capitalist enterprise possible. They are there because the capitalist parts of the economy (under state or private auspices) cannot absorb them.

All this is not to suggest that economic reform and global integration have not been important in China or India or that there has not been some unleashing of entrepreneurial energies in recent years; my plea is only to suggest looking more into the complex interaction of markets with the structural forces, positive and negative, that affect the lives of the poor.

China and India have now become poster children for market reform and globalization in parts of the financial press, even though in matters of economic policy toward privatization, property rights, and deregulation and lingering bureaucratic rigidities both countries have demonstrably departed from the economic orthodoxy in many ways. This has not escaped the attention of the Heritage Foundation, however. If one looks at the figures of the widely cited Index of Economic Freedom 2008 released by the Heritage Foundation, the ranks of China and India are quite low; out of a total of 157 countries, China's rank is 126th and India's 115th, and both are relegated to the group described as "mostly unfree," in a position much worse than many "moderately free" countries in Central and South America. Of course, not many have pointed out that the economic (particularly growth) performance of these two "mostly unfree" countries in terms of economic freedom seems to have been much better than that of most others.

Although there is no doubt that the period of socialist[3] control and regulations in both countries inhibited initiative and enterprise, it would be a travesty to deny the positive legacy of that period,[4] particularly in the pattern of state-controlled capitalist growth in China in recent years.

It is arguable that the earlier socialist period in China provided a good launching pad particularly in terms of

- a solid base of minimum social infrastructure (broad-based education and health care) for workers;
- a fast pace of rural electrification that facilitated growth of agro-processing and rural industrialization;
- a highly egalitarian land redistribution, which provided a minimum rural safety net that in the early years eased the process of market reform, with all its wrenching disruptions and dislocations;
- a system of regional economic decentralization (and career paths of Communist Party officials firmly linked to local area performance)—for example, county governments were in charge of production enterprises long before economic reforms set in (creating a pool of manufacturing experience, skills, and networks) and, drawing on this pool, the production brigades of the earlier commune system evolved into the highly successful township and village enterprises that led the phenomenal rural industrialization;

---

[3] It is arguable that India in the prereform period was not really socialist, except largely in political rhetoric. We'll ignore here the common confusion between socialism and bureaucratic statism (Franco's Spain had a lot of the latter, very little of the former).

[4] This legacy is often denied, and not just by Western commentators. The "new left" intellectuals of China (such as Wang Hui), in bemoaning the decline of ideological debates in China, have commented that in the minds of many Chinese people the twentieth century has been essentially reduced to its last two decades.

- the foundation of a national system of basic scientific research and innovation (even in 1980, spending on research and development as a percentage of GDP was higher than in most poor countries);
- high female labor force participation and education, which enhanced women's contribution to economic growth.

With respect to many of these, China's legacy of the earlier period has been much more distinctive than that in India. When I grew up in India, I used to hear leftists say that the Chinese were better socialists than we were; now I am used to hearing that the Chinese are better capitalists than we are. I tell people, only half-flippantly, that the fact that the Chinese are better capitalists now may be because they were better socialists then!

A major part of the legacy of the earlier period in both countries is the cumulative effect of the active role of the state in technological development. It is often overlooked that Chinese success in the international markets is not just in labor-intensive products like garments, toys, shoes, and wigs. Both China and India (but China much more than India) have succeeded in the export of products more sophisticated than is usually expected from countries in their respective per capita income range. This is remarkable and is primarily due to a sizable skill and technological base in both countries, enriched over the "slumbering" years by indigenous learning by doing, and nurtured by government policies of building domestic capabilities,[5] sometimes at the expense of static efficiency of resource allocation emphasized in traditional theories of comparative advantage. Take auto parts, for example. Protection of "local content" (of components) in automobiles, which is contrary to the orthodox trade policy prescription, was practiced in both countries, enabling their workers to learn the skills and reach international best practice now. There are, of course, many other cases where protection from foreign competition sheltered massive inefficiency. There are also

---

[5] In India, often those who are vocal about the adverse effects of Nehruvian Fabian socialism on the economy at the same time are proud of the contribution of the high-standard public-sector institutes of technology and management that Nehru promoted as part of state industrial and technological policy and whose students have now become technological and business leaders.

many cases of lingering government failures, for example in financial intermediation in China or social-service delivery in India.

Although there are recognizable elements of industrial policy and the "developmental state" in the case of China, we point out in chapter 6 crucial qualitative differences from the other East Asian cases: in contrast to the coordinated capitalism of Japan and South Korea (where the state presided over the coordination among private business conglomerates), the Chinese case can be, and has been, more aptly described as one of state-led capitalism from above and network (*guanxi*) capitalism from below to fit in the conditions of much weaker development of large private business in China; industrial policy has also been more diverse and diffuse in the context of regional variations and decentralized development in a continent-size economy; and foreign investment has played a much more important role in technological and organizational upgrading and international marketing than in the other East Asian countries.

The much more dramatic growth success of China compared to India (and of other East Asian countries earlier, under authoritarian regimes) does not in any way prove the superiority of authoritarianism over democracy in development, as we discuss in detail in chapter 10. We shall try to establish our claim that authoritarianism is neither necessary nor sufficient for development, and that the relationship between democracy and development is actually much more complex than is allowed in the standard discussion. Nor can one depend on the prospering middle classes to be sure-footed harbingers of democracy in China. In many cases the Chinese political leadership has succeeded in coopting the middle classes (including the intelligentsia, professionals, and private entrepreneurs) in its firm control of the monopoly of power, legitimized by economic prosperity and nationalist glory. Indian democracy derives its main life force from the energetic participation of the poor masses more than that of the middle classes.

China is widely, and rightly, acclaimed as a case of decentralized development, where in the 1980s and 1990s local industries under the control of local governments and collectives flourished. This is an aspect of industrialization that has largely bypassed India so far, even though important constitutional changes favoring devolution of power to local governments were carried out in the 1990s. But it is not widely known that with fast economic growth, and with local Party officials prospering in a reward system that emphasized their local economic performance (with access to profits of local collective enterprises and the power to privatize them), the central government in China is now finding it difficult to rein in these local officials, particularly in matters of land acquisition (often in cahoots with local commercial developers), environmental degradation, and violation of safety regulations relating to consumer products or work conditions in mines (often in collusion with local business). The chanting of the mantra of "harmonious society" by the central leadership has not yet been successful in curbing the capitalist excesses of local business and officialdom. The centralization of tax reform since 1994 has reduced the incentives (and capacity) of the local bureaucracy to serve social needs, particularly in interior provinces, and central transfers so far have not been adequate to compensate for this. The autonomy given to local public service units such as schools and hospitals has commercialized them to such an extent that the poor are often priced out of their services, as we show in chapter 8. Thus the lack of democratic accountability mechanisms is and will be particularly felt by the local people both in the type of economic growth pursued and the delivery of social services. China's vaunted regional decentralization, without democratic devolution, may now be a source of much discontent and may undermine the future sustainability of the economic growth it had earlier fostered.

On discontent, a part of the conventional wisdom in the media as well as in academia is that (a) globalization has led to rising inequality, and (b) the inequality-induced grievances, particularly in the left-behind rural areas of China, cloud the horizon for the future of Chinese polity and hence of economic stability. Since the effect of globalization on inequality is difficult to disentangle from that of other ongoing changes (for example, those of skill-biased technical progress due to new information and communications technology), the causal link between globalization and inequality is not always firmly established. Moreover, in China, provinces with more global exposure and higher growth did not have a greater increase in inequality than the provinces in the interior. The decline in agricultural growth in recent years in both China and India may also have something to do with the rise in aggregate inequality, independent of globalization. It should also be noted that the widely accepted statement in the media that inequality is greater in China than in India needs to be qualified. First, the usually cited data for China refer to income inequality, whereas most of the Indian figures relate to inequality of consumption expenditure (which in most countries is lower than inequality of income). From a recently available estimate of income inequality in India, it appears, as we show in chapter 7, to be much greater in India than in China. Second, inequality of income or consumption refers to inequality of outcome; socially (and morally) the more salient issue is that of inequality of opportunity, which in these poor agrarian economies is more often reflected in inequality of land and education. We'll show in chapters 3 and 7 that inequality of land and education is substantially greater in India than in China. Third, the usual income inequality figures do not correct for price differences across rural and urban areas and across regions; once corrected, the Chinese inequality of income is somewhat lower than the usually cited figure (in chapter 7 we'll cite evidence that if one takes into account cost of living differences between rural and urban areas and across provinces, the national Gini coefficient of income inequality in China increased from 0.29 in 1990 to 0.39 in 2004).

The relationship between inequality and social discontent is also rather complex. In chapter 10 we cite some evidence from China that the presumed disadvantaged rural people are not particularly upset by rising inequality. Rural people are often inflamed more by land seizures and toxic pollution than by inequality as such. Paradoxically, the potential for unrest may be greater in the hitherto booming urban areas.

In the subsequent chapters we discuss these and other aspects of the political economy of China and India in more detail and suggest that the story of their rise is more complicated and nuanced than it is made out to be in the standard accounts endlessly repeated in the media. Below is a short synopsis of some of the main issues discussed in the following chapters.

In chapter 2, we start with a brief description of the process of economic reform in the two countries and the associated remarkable increase in economic growth and total factor productivity in some sectors. (The association is easier to show than causation because of many other ongoing factors, and the other qualification, as we suggest in the appendix to the chapter, is that there are some reasons to doubt the accuracy of the growth statistics in both countries.) In general, reforms and growth in China have been deeper and have brought about an economic transformation particularly through labor-intensive rural industrialization, which is still largely missing in India. We explore some of the factors inhibiting labor-intensive industrialization in India and operating behind some particular features of the size structure of Indian industries (for example, bipolar distribution or the "missing middle"). We end with an analysis of the special institutional features of Chinese reform in terms of decentralized experiments and career incentives for local officials, which facilitated economic development and rural industrialization in a way that is rather unique, whereas the Indian system is more top-down and leaves few incentives for local officials to perform.

Chapter 3 is on the agricultural sector, which still employs nearly half of the workforce, even though there has been a precipitous decline in agriculture's relative contribution to national income in both countries (suggesting the large gap in productivity between farms and other sectors of the economy). Average farm size is declining in both countries, and while chemical and energy inputs to agriculture get more expensive, there is limited access to credit for small farmers to cover these costs (in China despite all the recent land legislation securing land rights of farmers, they are not yet allowed to mortgage their land rights to raise credit for agricultural investment). Meanwhile, with soil erosion and water depletion, the resource base of agriculture is steadily deteriorating in both countries. Both China and India have reduced their earlier antiagricultural bias in investment and protection policy, but China has

reduced the bias much more recently than India, where farmer lobbies have been politically more active and powerful for quite some
time. In fact, in India under political pressure of the farm lobby the
fiscal burden of water, electricity, and fertilizer subsidies to agriculture has mounted at the expense of public investment in rural infrastructure. As agriculture in both countries becomes intensive in
purchased inputs and more involved in outside market links, the
labor advantage of farm families is increasingly neutralized by the
disadvantage that small farmers face in credit, insurance, and marketing. The need for the latter will grow as agriculture diversifies
into cash crops and particularly horticultural and livestock products
that require cold storage and refrigerated transportation, insurance
against market fluctuations, and organized large-scale marketing.

In chapter 4 we start by noting the obvious, all too visible differences between China and India in the investment, construction, and
operation of crucial infrastructural services, particularly in power,
ports, roads, and railways. In all these sectors, political exigencies
and pressures of electoral populism in India keep user charges low,
even blowing the state budget in the process, hampering investment
incentives, and delaying the separation of government functions
from commercial operations, a matter in which China has advanced
much more. In addition, in China the decentralization of public finance even at the subprovincial level and close collaboration between local business and local government officials have enabled
much better funding and facilitation of local infrastructure projects
than in India. For many years now, infrastructure has been the key
bottleneck in Indian economic growth.

In chapter 5 we look at the pattern of saving and investment
in the two countries. Saving rates are high in both of them, with
household saving being higher in India, which is more than made up
for by higher public and enterprise saving in China. Populist pressure
on government spending keeps the fiscal deficit much higher in India, which hampers large-scale public investment in infrastructure.
In both countries, stringent financial regulations and state control
over banking have insulated them somewhat from external financial
contagion. In China, the state-controlled large banks dominate the

whole financial system, paying their depositors a below-market rate; nonperforming loans remain a significant burden; and allocation of capital remains severely distorted, particularly working against private enterprise. The Indian financial system is somewhat more balanced in terms of banking, equity, and bond markets as sources of formal finance, and it is better regulated and less saddled with bad loans. India's banking sector still leaves a large part of the economy with small enterprises seriously underserved, however, and with massive government borrowing, the cost of capital in the economy remains high. In both countries the informal sector remains the major (though sometimes more expensive or short-term) source of finance for most small producers; India's larger informal sector is reflected in the fact that India's informal lending market is much larger than China's.

In chapter 6 we look into the pattern of capitalism that is developing in these two countries, particularly in China. After many years of working in the shadows and using various subterfuges, private enterprise in China has come out in the open and the market mechanism is the main allocator of resources. The state is still predominant in the producer-goods sector and in transportation and finance. The state still controls the larger and often more profitable (high-margin, more monopolistic) companies in the industrial and service sectors. State-owned enterprises (SOEs) are often highly commercialized: in recruiting professional managers, broadening their investor base, and shedding their traditional social and political obligations, many SOEs do not conform to the usual stereotypes about SOEs. Ownership structures in China are often rather convoluted, but it is probably correct to say that now more than half of the economy is under mainly private ownership, though the private corporate sector is less vigorous and autonomous than in India. But the relationship between private business and the state is often rather clientelistic in China. In any case there is a new political-managerial class, which over the past two decades has converted its position of authority into wealth and power. In the relationship between the state and private business some analysts find an echo of the "developmental state" familiar from recent history in East Asia.

But we point out how in China (as well as India) the classic model of the developmental state does not quite fit.

In chapter 7, after describing the decline in poverty in both countries in recent years (dramatic in China, solid in India), we show that its relationship with market reform or globalization is more ambiguous than is usually claimed. The impact of growth on poverty reduction is weaker in India than in China, probably on account of initial conditions, including larger inequality (of opportunity) in India, owing to inequalities of land, education, and social status. The link between economic reform and inequality is also ambiguous and difficult to disentangle from the effects of other ongoing changes. There is limited evidence of significant intergenerational mobility in China, but not much in India.

In chapter 8 we examine the nonincome indicators of poverty and inequality, particularly relating to the social sector (health and education). In China, with the decline of the commune (and its basic services) and inadequate central fiscal transfers and charging of high fees for services rendered, access to these social services has declined seriously, particularly for the poor and in the interior areas. Within a rather short span of time China essentially moved from one of the most impressive egalitarian basic social-service systems to an effectively privatized (or user charge–financed) system, particularly in rural areas. India's social-service delivery system has remained dismal and inegalitarian throughout; for most of these services the poor in India often turn to private providers. In both countries, in spite of some major initiatives taken by the government in the past few years, some of the basic problems will linger as long as the system of incentives for the public providers is not restructured and as long as the local accountability mechanisms remain weak.

In chapter 9 we describe the alarming environmental conditions in both countries, focusing our attention primarily on the local environmental resources (such as water, forests, air, etc.). We cite a crude average score of comparative environmental performance in which China's aggregate score is slightly better than India's, but the performance of both countries is worse than the average in their respective per capita income categories of countries. The scores are abysmally low for both countries in sanitation conditions and indoor air pollution; they are also extremely low for pesticide regulation and biodiversity in India. The scores are relatively low for both countries in particulate matters in outdoor air in urban areas, in general air and water pollution (in terms of their effects on human health), and in contribution to climate change. Conditions are much worse in China than in India in industrial CO_2 emissions, air pollution (in terms of effects on ecosystem), and fisheries. The opposite is the case for environmental degradation in agriculture, where China's score is much better than India's. In both countries, economic growth aspirations are being tempered by increased consciousness of their environmental impact. Whether the Chinese central government's energetic countermeasures launched in recent years will succeed in making a big dent in the problems remains to be seen. The Indian countermeasures have yet not reached the scale of the Chinese countermeasures, but the environmental movement is more active as a watchdog in India.

The concluding chapter, chapter 10, brings together the threads of a comparative political-economy approach that have come up in the discussion of the various aspects of the economy in the two countries in the earlier chapters, focusing in particular on the governance issues that affect policy implementation and the pace and pattern of economic and political development. We start with a discussion of how democracy, as in India, unleashes both positive and negative forces for development, how there is some tension between the participatory and procedural aspects of democracy in matters of governance as well as in economic management, and yet authoritarianism is neither necessary nor sufficient for development. In India, the large number of poor in an assertive electorate have not always succeeded in focusing the attention of the politicians on the sustained implementation of programs to alleviate mass poverty or to deliver basic services such as education and health care. A heterogeneous society, riddled with social and economic inequalities and conflicts, makes collective action for lasting change difficult to organize and presents populist obstacles to long-term investment (that could cover, for example, India's serious infrastructural deficit) and reform. In a more homogeneous and less conflict-ridden society, the Chinese leadership can be more decisive and purposeful in pursuit of economic reform and long-term strategy, but in the absence of institutionalized checks and balances and of a rule-based system, there is a certain fragility in governance even in an otherwise strong state, and a danger of heavy-handed overreaction to crisis situations and of going off the rails. The decentralized governance structure, which has been a key to rural industrialization in China, has, in the absence of effective mechanisms of democratic accountability, limited the power of central government in reining in local officials from indulging in capitalist excesses in alliance with local commercial interests (resulting in environmental damage, violations of consumer product safety standards, or acceleration of economic inequality). In India, local democracy or self-government is still inadequately developed: regular elections at the district level and below are not followed up with effective accountability of governance to the local people in most areas (for funding and personnel, local governments are still hopelessly dependent on authorities above, apart from the problems of capture by the local power elite), and the delivery of essential social services and local public goods continues to be dismal. There are thus accountability failures in both countries, though their political contexts are different.

Chapter 2

Economic Reform and Growth:
Differing Patterns and Institutions

In both China and India economic reform started in the 1980s. In China it largely started in the form of experiments by some local farmers and conniving administrators. In 1978–1979, some farmers in Anhui province started testing the waters of the existing commune control over land use and effectively launched a movement of taking over land use as a private right of farmers. This spread very fast among farmers in neighboring villages and provinces, and within a few years the administration rationalized this evolving system all over China as what came to be called the household responsibility system, essentially a contracting system with individual farm households on their land use, subject to taxes and procurement of produce by the authorities. Along with a rise in procurement prices, the incentive for farmers of being able to retain much of the extra output they produce beyond that required to fulfill contracts with the state led immediately to a large increase in agricultural growth. As Lin (1992) points out, agricultural output grew at an annual average rate of 7.1 percent during 1979–1984, compared to 2.7 percent during 1970–1978. This included the effect of growth in traditional grains and the new freedom to reallocate land and labor to higher-valued nongrain crops. It is estimated that about half of output growth in this period can be attributed to the household responsibility system.

The reforms in the nonagricultural sector initially followed the same principles as in the agricultural sector. Apart from some contractual delivery to the state, industrial and commercial enterprises were given residual control, which boosted production incentives. This dual-track system, combining elements of both the earlier plan and the new market systems, operated even without a change in the state ownership of the enterprises. Thus this reform, by keeping some of the vested interests untouched at the initial stages, minimized the resistance to reform. But, as success gradually softened resistance, by the mid-1990s the two tracks were unified in favor of the market. The other reform was the increasing leeway given to collective, private, and foreign-invested firms. Through both of these reforms, market orientation of the economy grew by leaps and bounds. Experiments to attract foreign direct investment (FDI) were first proposed by some officials in Guangdong province in 1979. The Special Economic Zones attracted foreign investment at a time when private property rights generally were not protected by the legal system. From near-zero amounts at the beginning, FDI in China increased massively to become in time the second largest inflow to any country in the world economy.

The most dynamic part of the Chinese economy in the first two decades of reform were the township and village enterprises (TVEs), largely under the control of local governments, which provided the leadership in the labor-intensive rural industrialization of China. From less than 6 percent of gross domestic product (GDP) in 1978, TVEs' share climbed to 26 percent by 1996. Their average annual rate of growth was 28 percent in the 1980s (sometimes even higher in some of the coastal provinces). Sprouting under the shadow of the command economy, TVEs represented an institutional innovation (more a form of improvising) that employed the incentives of a market economy without privatizing ownership (at least in the initial stages). They benefited from the ability to retain most of the profits from the business, plentiful rural labor available locally, and cheaper credit from the local rural credit cooperatives (and other informal local sources) flush with the high savings of farmers (as the latter started prospering under agricultural reforms and as they increasingly felt secure against the danger of state confiscation of their surplus), and local officials often acted as informal guarantors

or sponsors of credit to the TVEs. But unlike state-owned enterprises (SOEs), they were not coddled or subsidized by higher-level
governments; failing TVEs were often not bailed out. In any case,
the lower-level governments or rural credit cooperatives often did
not have enough financial resources to bail out failing TVEs, even
if they wanted to do so. In this sense the budget constraint was
relatively "hard," so that not merely were the TVEs of different localities competing with one another, but the competition had some
teeth in it, as the local people had to bear the brunt of failed enterprises. The TVEs in the suburban areas often got subcontracts from
the SOEs, but over time they gave the hitherto protected SOEs
tough competition in markets where their products overlapped. In
due course, however, competition among the TVEs themselves and
outmigration of some managerial cadres reduced their profitability.
After the mid-1990s, as markets developed and as outright privatization was no longer taboo, the special advantages of local government ownership in terms of protection and access to resources
declined; in many of the TVEs the managers and associated local
officials openly staked their claim to ownership. Such insider privatization, of course, gave rise to many opportunities for manipula
tion and corruption.

Even though collective and private firms were the mainsprings
of growth, there were important reforms that made SOEs leaner and
more productive. In the 1980s, analogous to the household responsibility system in agriculture, regional and local governments experi-
mented with different kinds of "managerial responsibility systems,"
by which SOE managers often signed performance responsibility
contracts and were given more autonomy in decisions, financial
incentives tied to enterprise performance, and profit retention for
investment and worker bonuses.[1] In some cases, SOE managers were
selected by local governments through competitive auctions of com-
mitments to profit delivery. For an account of such SOE reforms of

[1] The profit orientation of SOEs also brought about a relaxation of their responsibility
to provide housing for workers. This led in the 1990s to a large program to subsidize buying of
apartments by occupants, in effect a massive privatization of the urban housing market, which
led to a construction boom.

managerial incentives and their positive effect on productivity, see Groves et al. (1995) and Li (1998).

The other route of SOE reform was outright privatization. From the late 1990s on, regional government officials had fiscal and other incentives (their career paths depending on the economic performance of local firms under ownership of all kinds) to privatize SOEs. According to a nationwide survey reported in Guo and Xu (2006), by 2005 more than two-thirds of Chinese regional SOEs were privatized and the top managers of three-quarters of these firms were the new owners.

All these reforms were associated with a high rate of growth in industrial output and total factor productivity (though we do not always have an econometric confirmation of the direction of causation from a particular reform to growth). As table 1 shows, industrial output grew at an annual rate of 9.3 percent between 1978 and 1993, and at 11 percent between 1993 and 2004. Total factor productivity (TFP) in industry grew at the annual rate of 3.1 percent in the first period and at twice that rate in the second period. China is now widely regarded as the manufacturing workshop of the world, but, as indicated in chapter 1, growth in output can be somewhat misleading for countries such as China (or India), where a large amount of manufacturing is assembling and processing materials and components: in 2004, China's share in the worldwide manufacturing *value added* was less than 9 percent, compared to Japan's 21 percent and the United States' 24 percent. In fact there is evidence that the growth in *value added* in the secondary sector was significantly higher in Taiwan and South Korea than in China in the first twenty-five years since the growth spurt started. See figure 1.

Although growth of exports and FDI in China contributed to employment expansion, technological and managerial upgrading, and disciplining of hitherto coddled inefficient enterprises, exports and FDI have not been the main driver of economic growth. Their direct net impact on GDP growth has been quantitatively modest compared to that of domestic investment or consumption, as shown by Branstetter and Lardy (2008)—see their figure 16.6. Even at the height of the global expansion of trade in the period 2002–2007, the

TABLE 1

Sources of Growth by Major Sector, 1987–2004 (Annual percentage rate of change)

Period		Output	Employment	Output per Worker	Contribution of Physical Capital	Land	Education	Factor Productivity
Agriculture								
1987–2004	China	4.6	0.3	4.3	2.3	0.0	0.2	1.8
	India	2.5	1.1	1.4	0.4	-0.1	0.3	0.8
1978–1993	China	5.2	0.9	4.3	2.5	-0.2	0.2	1.8
	India	2.7	1.4	1.3	0.2	-0.1	0.2	1.0
1993–2004	China	3.7	-0.6	4.3	2.1	0.2	0.1	1.8
	India	2.2	0.7	1.5	0.7	-0.1	0.3	0.5
Industry								
1987–2004	China	10.0	3.1	7.0	2.2		0.2	4.4
	India	5.9	3.4	2.5	1.5		0.3	0.6
1978–1993	China	9.3	4.4	4.9	1.5		0.2	3.1
	India	5.4	3.3	2.1	1.4		0.4	0.3
1993–2004	China	11.0	1.2	9.8	3.2		0.2	6.2
	India	6.7	3.6	3.1	1.7		0.3	1.1
Services								
1978–2004	China	10.7	5.8	4.9	2.7		0.2	1.9
	India	7.2	3.8	3.5	0.6		0.4	2.4
1978–1993	China	11.3	6.5	4.7	1.8		0.2	2.7
	India	5.9	3.8	2.1	0.3		0.4	1.4
1993–2004	China	9.3	4.7	5.1	3.9		0.2	0.9
	India	9.1	3.7	5.4	1.1		0.4	3.9

Source: *Bosworth and Collins (2007)*

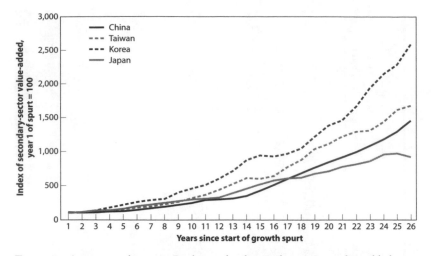

Figure 1. Asian growth spurts: Real growth of secondary-sector value added over twenty-six years. Source: Brandt, Rawski, and Sutton (2008)

increase in net exports contributed only about 15 percent of total real GDP growth in the period. As for trends in employment expansion, it should be noted that in recent years, particularly since the late 1990s, the composition of Chinese industrial output (and exports) has been shifting from low-tech labor-intensive products (such as garments, toys, wigs, and shoes) to higher-value products (such as computers, mobile phones, equipment, and instruments) using more advanced technology and inputs (often imported).[2] This will mean that the average skill- and capital-intensity of Chinese production is likely to go up, and job opportunities for unskilled workers may not expand at the same rate as before. This also means that some of the labor-intensive export goods may now shift to other, poorer countries where unskilled wage rates have gone up less. Of course, it is quite possible for China (being a large continental economy with

---

[2] While toys and shoes now account for less than 5 percent of China's total exports, machinery and transportation equipment now constitute nearly half of its total exports. Wang and Wei (2008) show on the basis of product-level data on exports from different cities in China that the main reasons for the increasing sophistication of China's export structure have to do with improvement in human capital and government policies in the form of tax-favored high-tech zones. But most high-tech exports from China are still made by foreign companies.

widely divergent regional conditions) simultaneously to pursue different types of industries in different areas for quite some time.

II

In India, after some deregulation of industry and trade liberalization in the 1980s, the pace of reform accelerated in the 1990s and afterward, involving abolition of most licensing of industry, most other restrictions on entry or capacity expansion for large firms, and quantitative restrictions on trade and exchange control; substantial scaling down of import tariffs and restrictions on foreign investment in most economic activities (with some exceptions in financial services, media, and retail trade); and significant lowering and restructuring of direct and indirect taxes (along with some streamlining of tax administration); and some reorganization of the public sector and opening of most areas to private investment that were formerly earmarked for the public sector (and a modest amount of privatization of public enterprises). The proportion of total trade (exports plus imports of goods and services) to GDP went up from about 16 percent in 1990–1991 to more than 45 percent in recent years. In China the rise has been much larger, from 21 percent in 1982 to more than 65 percent. (This rise in both countries has, of course, dampened with the current world recession.) In terms of simple average applied tariff rates, India's rates are still about twice China's,[3] and India's antidumping measures, some of them aimed against imports from China, have been among the most protectionist in the world. Nevertheless, the integration with the world economy has brought to India the discipline of market competition and associated firm reorganization, some foreign capital to many sectors (although the amount of FDI in China, even excluding "recycled" domestic investment, has been many times that in India), and some prominent acquisitions by Indian companies abroad that hit the headlines.

[3] The Chinese tariff rates are not merely very low; being generally near the World Trade Organization (WTO) bounds, they are also more predictable than those of India.

All these reforms have been associated with some acceleration of growth[4] in output and TFP, particularly sharp in the earlier part of the first decade of the twenty-first century (again, as in the case of China, an econometric analysis to establish the direction of causation from a particular reform to growth is rather rare). As table 1 shows, industrial output grew at the annual rate of 5.4 percent between 1978 and 1993, and at 6.7 percent between 1993 and 2004.[5] TFP grew at 0.3 percent and 1.1 percent in those two periods, respectively. Even though these rates are much lower than those in China, compared to the past these represent a significant advance for India. The Indian reforms seem particularly to have been associated with a more vigorous and competitive corporate sector.[6] As an empirical confirmation, on the basis of a panel dataset of large corporate firms Goldberg et al. (2008) show that the reduction in input tariffs led to large dynamic gains from trade over the period 1989–2003, through the import of new varieties of inputs leading to an explosion of new domestic product varieties. Of course, most of the economy is not in the corporate sector; about 45 percent of even nonfarm output and about 85 percent of nonfarm employment are outside the organized sector (public or private). It is, however, very likely that the reduction in controls and regulations and the increased leeway of market discipline and forces of competition may have unleashed entrepreneurial energies in both the formal and informal sectors and also forged additional links between the two sectors—links of subcontracting and consumer demand initiated by the formal sector. (I'd also speculate that the concurrent social changes in India, in the political rise of hitherto subordinate social groups after many centuries of social oppression, may also have played some role in this unleashing of energies.) But the relatively

---

[4] There is some disagreement in the literature about the timing of the "structural break" in the growth series.

[5] But manufacturing's share in total value added and employment did not change much between 1993 and 2004.

[6] The share of corporate investment in total investment has roughly doubled over the past two decades. But note that the official estimates of corporate investment (and savings) in recent years are likely to be overestimates on account of increasing data reporting and aggregating problems, as has been pointed out by the National Statistical Commission (2001).

low levels of education of workers and of female labor force participation, in addition to weak infrastructure, act as a damper on India's
growth, particularly compared to China.

We have discussed the industrial growth performance in the two
countries in the aggregate. For more detailed individual industry-
level productivity comparisons one needs to go beyond nominal figures in national currency units and convert them into a common
unit of measurement using properly constructed purchasing power
parities (PPPs). This is rarely done. But we do have some detailed
industry-level comparisons in PPP terms for the period 1980–2004
from Wu, Rao, and Lee (2008). They find that the comparisons are
different for four different industry groups. The first group consists
of machinery and equipment (including electrical, information/
communications, instrumentation/measuring, and transportation
equipment). In this group, industries in India were more productive than those in China at the beginning of the period but the
gap declined over time and even became negative in some cases.
The second group includes food and beverages, chemicals, building
materials, and metal products. In this group, industries in India re
mained on a par with those in China until very recently. The third
group includes textiles, apparel, wood products, leather and leather
products, rubber, plastics, and basic metals. Industries in this group
showed strong TFP growth performance in India relative to China
in the first half of the period but their relative performance has been
declining rapidly since the mid-1990s. The fourth group includes a
few sectors in which Indian industries have been performing better
in terms of TFP over the whole period, such as paper and printing,
or have caught up with and remained more productive than China,
such as tobacco, petroleum, and coke. A disaggregated analysis of
the reasons for such diverse performance across industries remains
to be done.

As shown in table 1, the most significant growth in India was in
the service sector; TFP in that sector grew from an annual average
of 1.4 percent in 1978–1993 to 3.9 percent in 1993–2004. Growth
in India has been described as service sector–led, whereas in China
it has been more manufacturing-centered (note, however, in table 1

TABLE 2

Growth in Components of the Service Sector (Percentages)

Period	Modern Services				Education and Medical	Traditional Services				Services Less Dwellings
	Total	Communications	Finance	Business Services		Total	Trade	Transportation	Other Services	
Share of Total Output in Services										
1960–1961	19	2	6	1	10	81	40	14	27	100
1980–1981	22	3	7	1	11	78	37	16	24	100
1993–1994	31	3	14	2	12	69	34	14	21	100
1999–2000	35	6	14	4	12	65	33	12	19	100
2004–2005	40	11	12	5	11	60	33	11	16	100
Annual Percentage Rate of Change										
1960–1980	5.7	6.9	5.9	3.4	5.5	4.6	4.5	5.6	4.3	4.9
1980–1993	9.0	7.1	12.3	9.8	6.6	5.4	5.6	5.4	4.9	6.3
1993–1999	12.6	20.3	9.3	28.0	10.6	8.9	9.8	7.5	8.6	10.1
1999–2004	10.5	23.8	5.7	11.4	7.1	6.5	7.9	5.7	4.3	8.0
Percentage Contribution to Total Services Growth										
1960–1980	1.1	0.1	0.3	0.0	0.5	3.8	1.8	0.8	1.2	4.9
1980–1993	2.0	0.2	0.9	0.1	0.7	4.2	2.1	0.9	1.2	6.3
1993–1999	3.9	0.7	1.3	0.5	1.2	6.2	3.3	1.1	1.8	10.1
1999–2004	3.7	1.3	0.8	0.5	0.8	4.2	2.6	0.7	0.8	8.0

Source: Bosworth, Collins, and Virmani (2007)

that in the first period, 1978–1993, even service-sector TFP grew faster in China[7] than India). One immediately thinks of the widely acclaimed performance of Indian software and other IT-enabled services. But it seems that in India's service sector not all of the growth in the period 1993–2004 can be explained by finance, business services, or telecommunications, where reform may have made a difference. Table 2 shows that a large part of the growth in the service sector, at a rate higher than that in manufacturing, was in the traditional or "unorganized sector" services, which even in the past decade formed about 60 percent of the service-sector output. These services, as noted in chapter 1, are provided by tiny enterprises, often below the policy radar, unlikely to have been directly affected substantially by the regulatory or foreign trade policy reforms. Thus the link between economic reform and growth in the leading service sector is yet to be firmly established, though it is possible that some informal service enterprises now act as subcontractors to large firms, and there may have been some spillovers of the communications revolution into the informal sector.

III

For various reasons, India has not yet succeeded in a massive expansion of labor-intensive manufacturing jobs of the kind that has transformed the economies of China and Vietnam. Which of these reasons are more important than others is not yet resolved at the level of rigorous empirical analysis. But most people agree on the problems of inadequate long-term finance for small firms and of infrastructural deficiencies in India (which we discuss in chapter 4). Many economists and businessmen also point to the debilitating effects of two long-standing policies in India: one relates to the reservation of a large number of products for small-scale industries (over the years the list of such products has dwindled—from more than eight

---

[7] Maddison and Wu (2008) have, however, questioned the labor productivity growth in the service sector in Chinese official data.

hundred to less than forty), and the other to rigid labor laws. Neither policy is found in China[8] or Vietnam. The policy of reservation is supposed to have prevented the utilization of economies of scale and rationalization of production in efficient large factories that can compete in world markets (particularly in terms of quality standardization and timely delivery), apart from acting as a built-in disincentive for a successful small firm to expand its operations. Small firms, while accounting for about 90 percent of manufacturing employment, contribute only about a third of total manufacturing output. The labor laws (particularly chapter V-B of the Industrial Disputes Act) make it very difficult to fire workers in large firms even when they are inefficient (or when the market declines) or even to redefine the job description of a given worker or to employ short-term contract labor; this discourages new hires by employers, induces capital intensity in production, and inhibits entry and exit of firms. The adverse effect of these two policies are particularly visible, critics point out, in the textile and garment sector, where China's success in recent years has far outstripped that of India (a country with a long history of textile production). Even after the dereservation of the garment sector in India from 2001 on and the lifting of the Multi-Fiber Agreement quotas in the United States and Europe, India's global market share has not dramatically improved, whereas China has already captured a dominant share.

Others have argued that the impact of these two policies are somewhat exaggerated. On account of various (overt and covert) exemptions, large companies have not always been kept outside the products under small-scale reservation. In textiles, there are clear economies of scale in spinning, but less in weaving, printing, and the manufacturing of garments. Indian spinning mills, both for cotton and for manmade fibers, have achieved international scale. That production scale did not matter in weaving and garments is evident from Japanese and Taiwanese experience, where textiles firms were

---

[8] One major restriction in the Chinese labor market, however, has been that a large proportion of the floating migrant worker population (estimated to be about 120 million in total) does not have housing registration (*hukou*)—a system that has only recently begun to be dismantled—and also faces other kinds of discrimination.

small but supported by large trading houses that secured economies of scale in marketing. The Chinese textile firms used to be state-owned and large, and there is an alternative hypothesis about the large size of those Chinese firms: China's huge state-owned textile factories may have partly reflected inadequate development of market-based interfirm relationships, which is evident in industrial clusters such as Tiruppur in Tamil Nadu. But now many of China's textile firms under joint venture and foreign ownership are relatively small. Chinese data suggest that nearly 60 percent of total sales and exports in the apparel sector is produced in relatively small firms (employing fewer than three hundred workers or having annual sales revenue of less than three hundred million yuan).

On labor laws, Dutta Roy (2004), in one of the few statistical studies at the industry level in India, found that over the period 1960–1961 to 1994–1995 the impact of job security regulations was statistically insignificant in fifteen of the sixteen industries studied: the rigidities in the adjustment of labor were about the same even before the introduction of stringent job security clauses in the law (the 1976 and 1982 amendments to the Industrial Disputes Act). More recent case studies of labor practices in ten states and nine industries over the period 1991–1998 by Deshpande (2004) also suggest that the Indian labor market is not as inflexible as it often is made out to be: many firms were able to change employment as they wanted or increase the share of nonpermanent (casual and temporary) workers.[9] Labor laws are implemented at the state level and it is well known that many state governments look the other way when they are openly violated—Jenkins (2000) has referred to this as an example of "reform by stealth." Court judgments on the interpretation of the laws also vary by states. One of the most detailed econometric studies of industrial growth based on state-level Annual Survey of Industries data in India for forty-two three-digit manufacturing industries for the period 1980–2004 is by Gupta, Hasan, and Kumar

---

[9] One problem in citing such data from existing firms, however, is the inevitable selection problem: one does not know about firms that did not enter the industry because of the stringent labor laws.

(2009)—although there are some problems with their particular measure of labor regulations and the estimation strategy used. They find that the impact of delicensing reforms (since 1985) has been highly uneven across industries: industries that are labor-intensive, use unskilled labor, and depend on infrastructure (or are energy-dependent) have experienced smaller gains in growth of value added from those reforms. States with less competitive product-market regulations have experienced slower growth and states with more inflexible labor-market regulations have experienced slower growth, particularly in labor-intensive industries. See figures 2 and 3.

The labor market may be more "flexible" in China than in India, but one should not exaggerate the difference in job security and benefits. As Cai, Park, and Zhao (2008) point out, until the late 1990s the government tightly restricted the dismissal of workers in China. Enterprises could dismiss no more than 1 percent of their employees each year, were barred from dismissing certain types of workers, and were expected to place dismissed workers in new jobs. Then at the end of 1990s came the large-scale layoffs from SOEs. But Giles, Park, and Cai (2006) find that during the period 1996–2001 a sig-

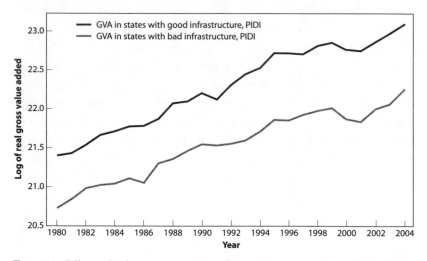

Figure 2. Effects of infrastructure on growth in registered manufacturing in India. Note: GVA = gross value added; PIDI = Physical Infrastructure Development Index. Source: Gupta, Hasan, and Kumar (2009)

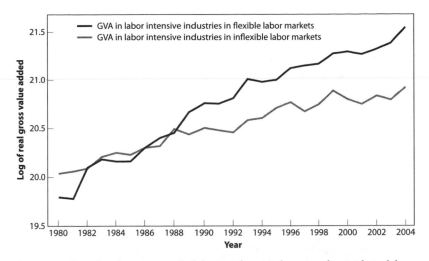

Figure 3. State-level variations in labor-market regulation and growth in labor-intensive industries in India. Source: Gupta, Hasan, and Kumar (2009)

nificant fraction of unemployed workers (nearly half in the case of older workers) had access to public subsidies (including post-layoff *xiagang* subsidies for three years, unemployment benefits at the end of those three years, and social assistance through the minimum living standard program). Since January 2008 a new labor law in China partially secures the tenure of longtime workers, but not so rigidly as in India.

The Indian trade unions of different political persuasions have been hostile to any labor market reform. Of course, they represent a tiny fraction of the total industrial labor force (nearly 90 percent of which are in the unorganized sector). Some labor laws, such as those that make union formation very easy (any seven people can start a union), and the lack of secret ballots in union decisions keep the labor movement weak and fragmented. On job security, there is ultimately no alternative to a package deal: allowing more flexibility in hiring and firing has to be combined with a reasonable scheme of unemployment compensation or adjustment assistance, from an earmarked fund to which employers as well as employees should contribute. No Indian politician has yet gathered the courage or imagination to come up with such a package deal.

It is also remarkable that the supposed procompetitive effects of deregulation and trade reforms have not yet made a big dent in industrial concentration in India (though there is some evidence of entry of new firms). Measures of industrial concentration (such as the Herfindahl Index) have not fallen much over time. Average price-cost margins increased in the 1990s across most two-digit manufacturing sectors.[10] China also experienced little major change in industrial concentration between 1993 and 2002, reflecting, as Brandt, Rawski, and Sutton (2008) suggest, the conflicting forces of opportunities for new entry and pressure for consolidation. The balance of these two forces varied across industries in China: for example, in recent years concentration increased among manufacturers of home appliances and beer, while both car and steel industries experienced an upsurge of new entrants.

According to the Organisation for Economic Co-operation and Development (2007), the Herfindahl Index scores of industrial concentration suggest that India's share of highly concentrated industries is more than three times that of China (or the United States). Such an anticompetitive environment, reinforced by persistent restrictive regulations in many states, is unlikely to have been favorable to industrial growth. The OECD's 2007 report provides a comprehensive measure of product-market regulations based on several indicators relating to state control, barriers to entrepreneurship and trade, and so on for many countries. By this measure, even after many years of considerable deregulation, product-market regulation is much more restrictive in India than in South Korea, Brazil, Mexico, or Turkey. The OECD also notes considerable variations in product-market regulation across twenty-one states in India (West Bengal is the most restrictive, Goa the least). Figure 4 provides a statistical depiction of the effects of state-level variation in product-market regulations on industrial growth.

The productivity effects of reforms are hampered by the peculiarities of industrial structure in India. India is rather unique in its size structure of nonagricultural enterprises, being dominated by

[10] See Balakrishnan and Babu (2003).

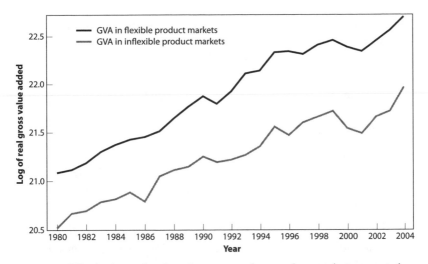

Figure 4. Effects of state-level variation in product-market regulations on industrial growth in India. Source: Gupta, Hasan, and Kumar (2009)

extremely small enterprises, with 87 percent of manufacturing employment being in microenterprises of fewer than ten employees (see figure 5). In China the informal sector had a shadowy existence in the prereform period and has started growing only very recently.

Even if one leaves out the petty household enterprises and confines oneself to manufacturing firms having six or more workers

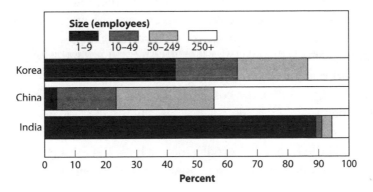

Figure 5. Size distribution of nonagricultural firms by employment. Unlike the data for China and India, the Korean data do not include all microenterprises and do not include services. Source: OECD Statistics on Enterprises by Size Class, computed from Indian Economic Census 2005 and Chinese Economic Census 2004

(including at least one hired worker), Mazumdar and Sarkar (2008) estimate on the basis of National Sample Survey (NSS) Establishment Surveys and Annual Survey of Industries (ASI) that in 2000–2001 about 42 percent of all manufacturing employment in India was in firms with six to nine workers (in 1984–1985 the percentage was 40). At the other end of the firm distribution, in firms employing 500+ workers the percentage was 23 (a decline from 30 percent in 1984–1985). This suggests two things: (1) there is a bipolar distribution—with what has been called a "missing middle"—in the Indian firm structure, particularly compared to China and other developing countries; and (2) the trade and deregulatory reforms and the slowly declining small-scale reservation, have gone along with a decline, not a rise, in the employment share of large firms. This is particularly important with the large productivity gap between the two ends of the bipolar distribution. In 2000–2001 labor productivity in the 500+ worker firms was about ten times that in the six- to nine-worker firms. This kind of productivity gap is larger than in most other developing countries (and has increased in India since the mid-1980s). Many factors may be responsible for the missing middle and the decline in the employment share of large firms. Labor laws, at least in some states, discourage hiring in large firms. But in most states this has not prevented large-scale retrenchment and layoffs, closures, and amalgamations. Infrastructural deficit, say in electricity, discourages the setting up of firms (or use of equipment that is prone to damage from erratic electricity supply and the associated voltage fluctuations) particularly in the middle of the size distribution, firms that cannot afford their own generators and, even if they can, find that the cost of generating power on a small scale is too high to be economically feasible. Highly inadequate access to credit has the same effect on small and medium firms.[11] The peculiarities of the Indian industrial structure have something to do with the much lower contribution to growth in India compared to China

---

[11] This is consistent with the wide interfirm gaps in marginal productivity of capital (which are larger in India than in China) that Hsieh and Klenow (2007) have estimated on the basis of ASI data.

from resource reallocation from low-productivity agriculture to the higher-productivity industrial sector.

IV

In one way Chinese economic reform is quite distinct from that in most countries, including India. The institutional foundations of Chinese reform have taken the form of regional experimentation and regional competition.[12] As indicated earlier, in many branches of economic activity, starting with agriculture, and then special economic zones, TVEs, management contracts in SOEs, privatization, and so on, new institutional arrangements were tried out first in local pockets and then, if successful, extended to other areas and given general political legitimacy. This experimental approach—in Deng Xiaoping's phrase "crossing the river groping for the stones"—has served China very well, diffusing political resistance to reform and convincing the undecided, in addition to updating the initial ideas of the reformers in a world of uncertainty. But this approach would not have worked if China had a less decentralized system. In the Soviet Union and pre-1989 Eastern Europe some of the experiments with liberalizing reforms failed on account of a top-heavy centralized system. In China the regions have substantial autonomy and relatively self-contained economies, with access to a variety of fiscal and nonfiscal resources. With a relatively low degree of interregional interdependence, it has been possible to isolate the impact if a regional experiment fails. India also has a low degree of interregional interdependence, and there have been a few cases of the spread of regional experimental success (one of the most prominent being that of the green revolution technology that first started in the irrigated agricultural areas of the northwest and then slowly spread to the rest of the country).

But regional decentralization is much more extensive in China and the vertical fiscal dependence of the regions on the national

[12] For a lucid and analytical account of this, see Xu (2008).

government is much less than in India; the national government is much less involved in local ventures (and therefore local failures), and the local governments have to take much more responsibility in China, leaving a lot of scope for local experimentation. India has much more of a top-down fiscal system. Of the total government expenditure in China more than half is made at subprovincial levels, compared to only about 5 percent in India. Local governments in India do not have the financial means for carrying out local experiments, and upper-level governments in India are more wary of such experiments, since they would be under pressure to bail out failed projects. In a democracy such pressures are inexorable; it is always difficult to cut losses and let go once a project starts.

Apart from having access to more fiscal resources (and kickbacks) if a project succeeds, local officials in China also have built-in career incentives within the Party, which uses rewards based on interregional competition to encourage local economic performance.[13] Li and Zhou (2005) provide evidence from the turnover data of top provincial leaders in China between 1979 and 1995 that the likelihood of promotion of provincial leaders in the Party hierarchy increases with their economic performance (while the likelihood of termination decreases). Thus decentralization of resources, rents, and responsibility, combined with centralized personnel control where local performance is rewarded by promotion, serves as a major engine of growth in China. The Indian governance system is quite a contrast in this respect: resources at the disposal of local governments are scanty, and officials are not rewarded for local economic performance. In fact, in general Indian officials serve in local areas for brief periods, often "on deputation" (with no institutional memory and no stake in local performance), and are averse to taking on high-risk, high-return projects because they do not share in the high return but do share in the blame if the project fails; so instead they bide time in their temporary posting, taking care not to rock the boat. A reputa-

---

[13] In measuring economic performance, local economic growth and targeted collection of particular tax revenues are weighted heavily; other criteria used include generation of employment opportunities and provision of public goods.

tion for administrative efficiency does play some role in promotion, but seniority trumps most other factors in career paths.

One possible pitfall of local autonomy and decentralization is that local governments may opt for local protectionism and barriers to interregional integration. This has not been absent in the Chinese case. There is some controversy on the importance of large internal market barriers in China; see, for example, Young (2000) and Poncet (2005). Poncet finds increasing provincial border effects on trade over the 1990s, despite all the liberalization. But Fan and Wei (2006) provide credible evidence to the contrary. They show that even for the raw industrial materials that are most under the control of local monopolies, prices are converging across regions. According to them, the law of one price holds in general, and for products other than services the price dispersion across regions is similar to that in the United States. There are no comparable data for different types of products in India, but whatever data exist do not suggest that internal market integration is any better in India than in China. This is particularly the case for agricultural products, whether in their primary or processed state, as there are many restrictions on free sale of these products in different parts of India. Virmani and Mittal (2006) provide some evidence that price dispersion across states in some basic commodities has declined in the past decade. Nevertheless, after nearly sixty years of constitutional federalism, India is as yet nowhere near being a common market.

In this chapter we have briefly described the main features of economic reform in the two countries and the associated increase in economic growth and TFP in different sectors. In general, reforms and growth in China have been deeper and have brought about economic transformation particularly through labor-intensive rural industrialization, which is still largely missing in India. We have explored some of the factors that inhibit labor-intensive industrialization in India and that lie behind some particular features of the size structure of Indian industries. Finally, we have analyzed the special institutional features of Chinese reform in terms of decentralized experiments and career incentives for officials, which uniquely facilitated economic development.

Appendix: Are the Growth Rates Really That High?

It is not widely known that the official income data on the basis of which the high growth rates of China and India are bandied about are prone to substantial errors and in many respects are quite shaky, even though both countries have competent and reasonably well-functioning statistical bureaucracies. There are serious problems with the price deflators used, the methods of estimation of output in the informal sector and household enterprises, and with the coverage of new goods and quality improvements (particularly salient with the opening of the economy), apart from political incentive problems in data reporting from lower levels (especially in China, where party cadre rewards are linked to local growth performance with a built-in incentive for overreporting). In India at least there is much more open discussion and critical examination of data limitations.[14]

It is generally recognized that there may be an upward bias in Chinese official data on rates of growth, particularly attributable to the price deflator used for the industrial sector and the fact that earlier a large part of income was received in the form of noncash subsidies, which may not have been fully entered in income accounting. Official prices may have artificially exaggerated the relative price of fast-growing manufactures.[15] Output data for township and village enterprises may also have mixed current and constant prices, leading to an upward bias to growth measures for inflationary years. It is also possible that, unlike in the later years, in the earlier years the lower-than-market procurement prices have been used in valuation of home-consumed grain, thus underestimating income and overstating the growth rate over the years. In comparison with Indian data, Chinese official income data are particularly problematic when projected backward. At purchasing power parity (using Penn World Table 2000

---

[14]Also, China is still in the process of converting its statistical reporting system from the old Soviet-style Material Product System to the international system of Standard National Accounts.

[15]Fan, Perkins, and Sabin (1997) show that because planned pricing undervalued agriculture, the official estimates of sectoral share may understate the decline of agriculture since 1980.

prices), official per capita GDP in China would be as low as half of that in India in 1978 (and 40 percent of that in India in 1952), which most people would find difficult to believe. If instead you accept the adjustments to the Chinese official data made by Maddison and Wu (2008), assume that India and China had roughly equal per capita incomes in 1952, and use 2000 PPP for Indian official data, then Heston's (2008) estimates suggest that the annual rate of growth in per capita income in China in the period 1978–2003 was a little below 7 percent, which is lower than the official rate but still quite impressive over a quarter century by historical standards in any country (twice that of the Indian growth rate in the period). The revised PPP figures from the 2005 International Comparison Program coordinated by the World Bank have substantially brought down the per capita income levels of both countries (by about 40 percent), but it is not yet clear what implications this has for the growth rates.

Since the informal sector is a much larger part of the Indian economy than of the Chinese, the problems of measuring output in this sector are particularly acute for India. The long-standing undermeasurement of the service-sector output in China has not yet been fully corrected. In India as well, the service sector, which now contributes 55 percent of GDP, has special problems in output measurement and the price deflators used, as the National Statistical Commission has highlighted.[16] In the absence of further research it is not clear how these problems will bias the growth rates: if the extent of over· or underestimation of value added remains the same over time, the growth rates will not be affected.[17]

[16] If the service-sector price deflator were to grow at the same rate as the GDP deflator (as it did over the forty years 1951–1991), the service-sector growth rate in recent years would have been significantly lower than the official rate reported. For some additional problems in the indirect procedures of estimating the value added by the large "unorganized" segments in this sector, see Srinivasan (2008).

[17] Nagaraj (2008) suspects that there is some overestimation in the growth rates of the formal service-sector output in communications and business services, and in the private corporate sector of the economy in general.

Chapter 3

Agriculture: Still the Most Crowded Sector

China and India are two of the ancient agrarian economies of the world, supporting massive numbers of (mostly poor) people. Agroclimatically they are, however, quite different. India is the land of the monsoons, which means torrential rain concentrated in very short periods of the year, whereas in China the average rainfall (at least in the more settled parts of the country) is somewhat more evenly distributed over the year. As Cai and Rosegrant (2007) point out, in China the pattern of rainfall follows more closely the pattern of solar radiation, providing conditions favorable for crop growth; India lacks a similarly synchronized pattern of precipitation-radiation. The average evapo-transpiration rates are much higher in the Indian river basins than in the Chinese. Reservoir storage of the water supply in China is almost five times that in India, where groundwater pumping (at almost twice the rate of China) partly substitutes for surface-water storage. India also has large tracts of semiarid areas where irrigation is very costly and thus scanty. China has had more cultivated land under irrigation for many decades.

The Chinese rice yield per hectare has been higher than India's for many centuries. In recent decades the green revolution (adoption of high-yielding varieties of seeds, adapted by national research systems from international technology) has significantly improved the yield for the main grain crops in both countries. On top of that, the move from the agricultural collectives to the household responsibility system in China led to a dramatic rise in productivity in the initial years of the 1980s, as noted in chapter 2. Overall, as table 1 in chapter 2 shows, total factor productivity (TFP) in agriculture grew at an annual rate of 1.8 percent in the period 1978–2004 (0.8 percent in India). In absolute comparison, Chinese productivity per hectare is double that of India in rice (and some oilseeds), and one and a half times that of India in wheat.

Higher saving in China has allowed more investment in agriculture, and the greater spread of literacy among farmers, a more equitable distribution of land (allowing better alignment of production incentives with cultivation rights), more intensive population control, and the spectacular success of rural industrialization, relieving some of the pressure on land, have all helped to raise China's productivity in agriculture above India's. Yet, according to official data, nearly 45 percent of the Chinese labor force is still in agriculture[1] (even though agriculture's contribution to GDP is approximately 12 percent). In India the corresponding percentage of the labor force is around 55 (and agriculture's contribution to GDP is approximately 18 percent).

The large discrepancy in both countries between agriculture's contributions to GDP and to total employment is, of course, a main source of the urban-rural disparity in income. Average farm size is declining in both countries, and while chemical and energy inputs to agriculture (such as fertilizers, pesticides, electricity, and diesel) get more expensive, there is limited access to credit for small farmers to cover these costs. The relatively limited spread of education in rural areas has meant that children in peasant families are less equipped to exploit the opportunities that globalization and market reform are opening up throughout the economy. Meanwhile, with soil erosion and water depletion, the resource base of agriculture is steadily deteriorating in both countries.

---

[1] There is some doubt about this official figure, largely arising from the fact that many people have migrated to the urban areas but are still registered in their villages. Brandt, Hsieh, and Zhu (2008) cite a rural household survey dataset for ten provinces, according to which the primary-sector employment share in the total was only 32 percent in 2004.

II

In China, market liberalization in agriculture came several years after decollectivization. The compulsory quota and procurement system was steadily abandoned by the government, and the share of farm produce sold in open markets increased from 6 percent in 1978 to about 80 percent by 1993. Then government involvement in agricultural markets mostly ended with China's entry into the World Trade Organization (WTO) in 2001 (except for some lingering state grain and cotton marketing enterprises in some provinces). The agricultural input market (for example, that for fertilizers) was also liberalized as part of that entry. In general, China has moved away from taxation toward net subsidization of grain producers (within WTO limits) in the past few years. As figure 6 suggests, both China and India have reduced their earlier antiagricultural bias (looking at the degree of sectoral assistance in agriculture versus nonagriculture, measured from product prices taking into account domestic and border taxes and subsidies), but China has reduced the bias much more recently than India (where farmer lobbies have been politically more active and powerful for quite some time).

Market and trade liberalization in agriculture also led to a shift in the production pattern from land-intensive products such as cereals to more labor-intensive products such as horticultural (fruits, vegetables) and livestock products. In general, the share of higher-valued cash crops, horticultural goods, livestock, and marine products in total output has shot up in the past two decades. It is remarkable, for example, that between 1990 and 2004 China increased vegetable production every two years by the equivalent of the total vegetable output of California. In both India and China, however, government policy emphasizes national food security, which limits specialization in nonfood crops.

In India the green revolution started in the northwestern part of the country in the mid-1960s, and slowly spread to other parts, particularly areas with plentiful groundwater and where access to credit and subsidized electricity or diesel encouraged the pumping of this water. But by the late 1980s this technology largely ran out of steam.

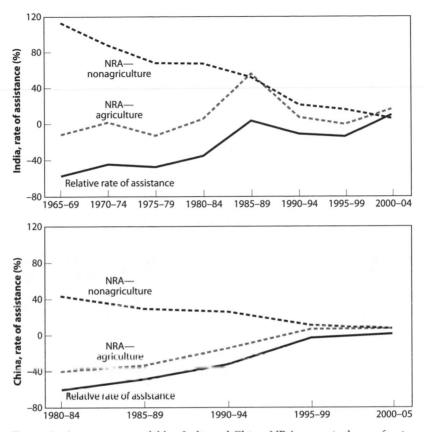

Figure 6. Assistance to tradables, India and China. NRA = nominal rate of assistance. Source: *World Development Report 2008* on the basis of Anderson (2009)

To sustain growth, governmental expenditures on input subsidies and support prices for grains increased. India's food subsidy (which is largely made up of the difference between the price at which the government procures grains and the lower price at which it distributes them through a highly inefficient public distribution system) was less than 0.2 percent of GDP in 1980, but this multiplied several times over the next quarter century. In the same period in China, food subsidy[2] as a percentage of GDP went *down* from about 2.3 to

---

[2] The estimate of food subsidy in China includes that for edible oil, sugar, cotton, and meat, apart from grains.

less than 0.5 percent (partly, no doubt, because of the much faster rise of GDP in China than in India). The rising volume of subsidies for fertilizers, power, and water in India encourage wasteful and environment-damaging use of resources (leading to groundwater depletion and soil degradation), apart from the fiscal burden involved. China also underprices its (surface) irrigation water, but its average water charge per hectare is more than four times India's.

The terms of trade between agriculture and manufacturing in India improved between the early 1980s and the middle of the first decade of the twenty-first century.[3] This has stimulated increased private investment in agriculture, particularly in the high-demand nongrain products. But public investment in rural infrastructure (irrigation, rural electrification, rural roads) and provision of extension services have declined. In a way, the mounting government spending on subsidies has crowded out public investment. For a suggestive plotting of the trend see figure 7. Public spending as a percentage of agricultural GDP in 2000–2002 was about four times larger on subsidies than on public investment (whereas at the beginning of the 1980s the latter was larger than the former). Most of the subsidies are given in the name of the majority of poor farmers and consumers. But most of the subsidized food does not reach the poor, particularly the rural consumers in the poorest states (where the public distribution system is weak and corrupt). And most of the producer subsidies go to the big farmers, and, in the case of the fertilizer subsidy, nearly half goes to uncompetitive fertilizer manufacturing companies. A study in Andhra Pradesh provides evidence that only 5 percent of the total electricity subsidy goes to the overwhelming majority of poor farmers who cultivate land less than two hectares.[4] The governments of Andhra Pradesh and Punjab spend more on electricity subsidy alone than their total budgets for health or general education.

The need for increased public investment is now generally recognized by the Indian government. But the magnitude of public in-

---

[3] In China, it seems, over roughly the same period the agricultural terms of trade fluctuated quite a bit, going up in the 1980s but declining both in the early and the late 1990s, and slowly improving since then.

[4] See Vashisht et al. (2006).

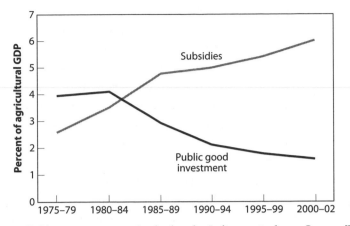

Figure 7. Public investment and subsidies for Indian agriculture. Source: *World Development Report*, on the basis of data in Chand and Kumar (2004)

vestment is only a small part of the problem. The bulk of public investment in agriculture is for surface irrigation, but most projects are afflicted by long delays and cost overruns and are inadequately linked with sustained efforts to stimulate local-level management and maintenance. As a result, much of the irrigation potential generated (or waiting to be completed) at great expense does not bear fruit in improving productivity. As in many other contexts in India, autonomous local-level management of common resources and coordination of community efforts at rainwater harvesting and watershed development (along with water demand management through locally suitable water-efficient agronomic practices) remain part of a crucial governance challenge. In any case, development thinking and popular enthusiasm have moved away from gigantic irrigation projects requiring large investment and displacement of people and toward water-resource management and conservation.

Even in China, where public protests against irrigation projects' impact on the ecosystem and on displacement of people are more subdued, there is a slow movement in development thinking (though not always reflected in official action) away from the gigantism of projects like the Three Gorges Dam and toward management reform and local water institutions. In the socialist period the state mobilized large amounts of resources and people in various irrigation projects. After the rural decollectivization of the late 1970s, as was the case with other social services, there was a decline in the local governments' financial ability to invest in local water storage and delivery systems. Also, with the new arrangement of individual cultivation rights, farmers' individual incentives to maintain and invest in these public or community systems were ambiguous at best. After 1990, village surface-water management largely passed to water-user associations and contracting with individuals on maintenance tasks and water-saving incentives. In groundwater management, particularly in northern China, the system has gradually shifted from collective tubewell ownership to private ownership. This presents to China a major problem that has been salient in Indian groundwater management: how to politically and legally establish that underground aquifers are part of common pool resources where individual use rights have to be limited so that overextraction is discouraged, and how to enforce this effectively. As in India, Chinese local governments have found it difficult to meter or monitor energy use or collect fees from numerous small farmers. Nevertheless, cost recovery has been in general better in China under a less top-heavy water bureaucracy than in India.

III

Producer incentives from land rights have been quite different in the two countries. China, of course, has had a checkered history of land tenure over the past sixty years or so. When the commune system of agriculture gave way to the household responsibility system, China carried out one of the world's most egalitarian distributions of individual land-cultivation rights, with each family in the village getting more or less an equal size plot of land, subject to differences in family size and regional average. This led to an alignment of individual production incentives with land-control rights, which led to a spurt in agricultural productivity in the early 1980s; by providing a floor to rural income or food consumption, it also provided a cushion against extreme poverty (something that is woefully lacking in India, where there are tens of millions of landless or near-landless poor people).

But there are some lingering ambiguities in land rights in China, arising out of the fact that the village collective still formally owns the land and periodically reallocates it to align with life-cycle changes in families and public, often commercial, development purposes. There is also the issue of transferability of land rights. These ambiguities can clearly provide disincentives to long-term investment in land. Over the past two decades the Chinese government has adopted some policies and laws to respond to these issues: the 1993 policy directive to lengthen the farmers' tenure to thirty years; the 1998 Land Management Law, which formalized this; the 2002 Rural Land Contracting Law, which provided legal remedies for any violations that the farmers faced; and the 2007 comprehensive Property Law, which converted the farmers' contractual rights into more formal property rights. In October 2008 new rules on transfer and exchange of land-use rights were announced. These rules, apart from facilitating land consolidation, may particularly ease trading of nonarable land (strict limits on transfer of arable land remain).

In the absence of an independent judiciary, these successive formalizations are more political than legal indicators of the intention of the central leadership. But because the implementation of these directives and laws is in the hands of local officials, their effectiveness varies greatly in different regions. For example, in the 1980s and 1990s, the average number of administrative reallocations per village was much larger in Liaoning province than in Sichuan; there was hardly any reallocation done in Guizhou province. The 2002 Rural Land Contracting Law prohibits land readjustments within the thirty-year period except under "special circumstances," which are, of course, interpreted elastically by local officials. Land-use rights are transferable in lease contracts and heritable. This has encouraged land lease-out to people with more ability (and farmhands and farm animals) and interest in agriculture, although the percentage of land under such (sub)tenancy was rather low until very recently. The official land tenancy figures in India are higher. This is in spite of the fact that tenancy is prohibited in several states in India, and the official estimates of tenancy figures[5] are likely to be underestimates, as prohibition of tenancy drives some of the tenancy contracts underground. As with Indian tenants (whose terms of lease are often oral, except in states such as West Bengal, where tenancy rights are to a large extent registered), Chinese farmers have not mostly been allowed to mortgage their land rights to raise credit for agricultural investment. As mentioned earlier, until very recently private land sales were prohibited in China; in India also the private agricultural land market is not very active partly because large landowners often derive many kinds of benefits (not all of which have to do with cultivation) from holding on to the land, and potential small buyers find it difficult to raise the money in the credit market.

The most contentious issue in Chinese villages over the past few years has been the arbitrary way local village officials have taken away land from farmers, with highly inadequate compensation, to use for commercial development. This was a lucrative source of "extrabudgetary revenue" (now restricted) for local governments and of corrupt deals between local officials and commercial developers. This has fueled thousands of local disturbances and incidents of peasant unrest each year. The 2007 Property Law establishes a new compensation standard linking compensation to adequacy in maintaining the affected farmers' long-term living standards. How this will be actually implemented at the local level remains to be seen. (Already there have been reports that local officials now, instead of seizing the land, force the peasants to lease their land to the developers.) In India also there have been many flashpoints of peasant unrest and violence in the past few years when the government tried to acquire land for industrial, mining, or infrastructural purposes. Highly inadequate compensation and inefficient and scanty efforts to resettle and redeploy the displaced farmers have been at the fore-

---

[5] The percentage of cultivated land under tenancy in India in 2002–2003 was about 7 percent according to National Sample Survey data. For China, Rozell et al. (2002) suggest that in the mid-1990s about 2.9 percent of cultivated land was under tenancy. Since then the percentage has gone up considerably.

front of political debates and agitations. The Indian government is trying to change the Land Acquisition Act of 1894 to redress some of these grievances.

The land distribution in China remains much less unequal than that in India. The Gini coefficient of distribution of land (in terms of operational holdings[6]) in rural India was 0.62 in 2002; the corresponding figure in China was 0.49 in 2002.[7] The Gini coefficient is so much higher for India partly because a much larger percentage of rural households are landless in India. When land is the major form of wealth for most people in these two agrarian economies, equality of land distribution matters not just for equity and social justice but also for production efficiency. It has been observed all over the world that, particularly in traditional agriculture, smaller farms are usually characterized by higher land productivity. This is primarily because small farmers have a labor advantage: they have access to family workers (for example, women) who for various social and economic reasons often would not offer themselves in the outside wage labor market (which the large farmers draw on for their hired labor); and outside hired labor requires supervision costs, which are usually unnecessary for family labor.

But as agriculture in both countries has become intensive in purchased inputs (such as fertilizers) and more involved in outside market links, this labor advantage is increasingly neutralized by the disadvantage that small farmers face in credit,[8] insurance, and marketing. The need for the latter will grow as agriculture diversifies into cash crops and particularly horticultural and livestock products, which require cold storage and refrigerated transportation, insurance against market fluctuations, and organized large-scale marketing. In

---

[6] In terms of land ownership, the Gini coefficient in India is much higher, 0.74.

[7] This, of course, does not correct for land quality. Land quality is partly taken into account in its valuation when land is included in the Assets and Liabilities Survey. According to this survey by the NSS, the Gini coefficient of ownership of asset distribution in rural India was 0.63 in 2002, while the corresponding figure for China was 0.39 in the same year. For the Chinese estimate, see Shi, Wei, and Jing (2005). The Indian estimate is by the author. The land Gini estimate for China cited in the text is from Khan (2004).

[8] The differential advantage of large farmers in raising credit may be less in China than in India, as land is not yet usable as collateral in China.

both China and India the average farm size, already small[9] (smaller in China), is declining, and in many cases it is falling below a minimum economically viable size, particularly from the point of view of the new needs of diversified production and coping with market and ecological risks.

Marketing in particular has large economies of scale, for which one needs large-sized marketing organizations. In India in the name of protecting the numerous small farmers from exploitation by large traders, an inefficient bureaucratic setup created an elaborate and antiquated structure of regulations that hurt farmers through monopoly purchase by state-appointed commission agents who then sold to wholesalers. Some states are now trying to reform this monopoly system. Other restrictions on storage, distribution, and movements of produce are being relaxed. Some supermarket chains are trying to establish direct buying from farmers but have so far been less successful than in China, primarily due to political opposition from small traders and grocers and state commission agents. In foreign trade of agricultural products there has been a general reduction of applied average tariffs, elimination of quantitative restrictions, and weakening of the monopoly of state trading agencies.

For high-value produce, some successful examples of contract farming between farmers and corporate firms (particularly in dairy, poultry, and food processing) are coming up in India, but they are still few and far between (and in some states illegal). In China, Guo, Jolly, and Zhu (2007), on the basis of a survey of farmers in thirteen provinces (most data are from three provinces in eastern China), find that about one-fifth of farmers have entered into contract farming with agribusiness firms (called "dragonhead-driven companies"), and many others would like to join. Farmers identify price stability and market access as the key advantages to such contracts. In both countries the model of cooperative marketing has been recommended to improve small farmers' bargaining power as they face large corporate giants and to coordinate standardization and quality issues.

---

[9] In both countries, the average farm is not merely small but fragmented into several parcels.

This model may also help the corporate firms or retailers reduce their transaction costs in supply-chain management. In the Chinese survey about a fifth of the agribusiness firms use a cooperative as the intermediary between themselves and farmers. For a long time, the most successful example of cooperative marketing in India has been the National Dairy Development Board in Gujarat (which is now branching out into fruits and vegetables as well). But there are not too many such examples; cooperatives of small farmers in India are often anemic and easily turn into conduits for bureaucratic subsidies or are captured by large farmers.

In both countries, without a substantial overhaul of the credit and marketing systems and a restructuring of the institutions around water and land management, small-scale agriculture, in which hundreds of millions of poor people are crowded, will not be able to cope with the growing demands of markets or escape the trap of low productivity.

Chapter 4

Infrastructure: The Dazzling Difference

To most outside visitors the difference between the two countries in the quantity and quality of physical infrastructure is immediately visible: the glitzy airports, multilane highways, gleaming skyscrapers, urban transportation, ports, high-speed trains, and so on all point to the indubitable fact that China is clearly far ahead of India in this matter. It is, however, important to probe the factors underlying this much too glaring difference, since they indicate some of the structural differences in the political economy and civil society of the two countries. This is particularly the case when one keeps in mind that in the beginning of the reform period of the early 1980s, even as late as 1990, India was ahead of China in terms of the standard indexes of many of the infrastructural facilities. (For example, at the beginning of the 1990s India's highway and railway infrastructure was ahead of that in China in terms of route kilometers.) That China could do this giant leap in a short span of years while India, with its creaking infrastructure, fell behind indicates major differences not merely in government spending patterns (China's infrastructural spending as a proportion of GDP has been more than twice as much as India's—see figure 8) but also in the institutional-political environment and practices in finance and management in the two countries.

The most important infrastructural bottlenecks in India involve power and transportation.

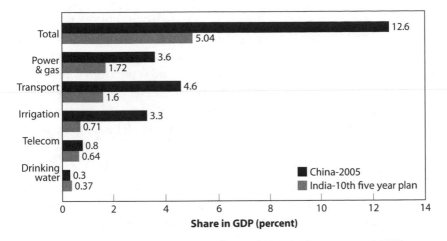

Figure 8. Infrastructure investment, China and India (percentage of GDP).
Source: Gupta, Hasan, and Kumar (2008)

II

Power

In both countries generation, transmission, and distribution of power are in the hands of enterprises that are predominantly state-controlled. But China has advanced a great deal more in commercializing the operations, first at the provincial level in 1987, and then at the national level in 1997. The emphasis is on the autonomy of the power companies, cost recovery, competition among generating companies, cost-based pricing of transmission and distribution, and strict enforcement of payment by consumers. The average rate of return on equity in power-generating companies was about 12 percent in 2007, and thus there is ample incentive for investment. The development of the electricity sector has more or less kept pace with the rapid industrial growth in the economy. Industry consumes about three-quarters of the power, while agriculture and residential consumers together take up only about 14 percent. There is very little power theft, and loss in transmission is only about 7 percent of total output, largely on account of technical factors.

All this is in sharp contrast to India, where enormous financial losses of distribution companies resulting regularly in large fiscal drain on government coffers; severe underpricing, under populist political pressure, of electricity to farmers and residential consumers (who account for more than half of the total electricity units sold); and large-scale power theft (in which consumers and employees of public distribution companies are complicit) are all rampant in many states, even though in recent years sporadic reforms have improved matters somewhat. Problems of cost recovery (and default on payments owed to power generators) act as a formidable disincentive for investment (private or public) or market-based risk-assessed finance. Power supply is erratic, with large voltage fluctuations (often damaging equipment and interrupting production runs in factories). This particularly hurts small producers. Most middle and large firms have their own "captive" power generators, of course driving up costs on account of the small scale of generation. The cost of power for manufacturing is reported to be about 35 percent higher in India than in China. A recent study by the accounting firm KPMG has estimated that a company can expect about seventeen significant power shutdowns per month in India, whereas in China the corresponding number is about five. According to a study by Goldman Sachs, the percentage of sales value lost due to power outage for Indian business is nearly six times that in China. Unlike in China, the pace of power generation in India has not kept up with the growth rate in the economy, and energy shortfalls have increased in recent years.

The major power reform legislation, the Electricity Act of 2003, which attempts to inject some competition and efficiency into the sector, has not yet been successful, by and large, in commercializing the operations of the state electricity boards (SEBs) and state government distribution companies, making them financially viable customers for potential investors in electricity generation, or in breaking their monopoly (in buying and distributing power). The regulations for third-party access to electricity transmission have not yet been implemented. After years of reform funding for metering and audit, metering of consumer use and collection efficiency are still dismally low. Large negative rates of return on capital employed in SEBs have been persistent. Subventions from state budgets to cover losses of SEBs have often exceeded 10 percent of the state gross fiscal deficit; this is apart from provision of loans and loan guarantees by the state governments. Aggregate technical and commercial (ATC) losses (including theft and nonbilling) were about 37 percent in 2004–2005 for the country as a whole (larger in some northern Indian states). The performance variations across states are large: an index of revenue orientation (composed of factors such as ATC losses, collection efficiency, gap between the average revenue realization and the average cost of supply, the ratio of commercial and industrial segments that cross-subsidize the agriculture and domestic customer segments, etc.), computed by Patel and Bhattacharya (2008), is relatively high for states such as Orissa, Himachal Pradesh, Maharashtra, and West Bengal, and very low for states such as Bihar, Uttar Pradesh, Karnataka, and Haryana.

Highways

China's progress in building highways has been simply phenomenal. In 1988, China had barely one hundred kilometers of expressways; within ten years, the total length of China's expressways had become second only to that of the United States, and rose to 60 thousand kilometers by 2009. In the 1990s China increased its spending allocation for highways by a factor of nearly forty. In freight transportation, total ton-kilometers grew at almost as fast a rate as GDP. Most of the investment was made by local governments (out of highway maintenance fees and construction fund) or firms controlled by local governments. In road transportation, bank loans backed by government guarantees and toll revenue were the most important source of funds. Funds raised by highway construction enterprises (including toll collection) were also a significant source. Corruption (in the form of kickbacks and bid-rigging) was, of course, rampant in highway construction. There was often collusion between the local government regulator and the regulated construction company, in matters of land acquisition, securing loans, and the approval of toll rights and rates.

In India, only in the late 1990s was a major and bold initiative in constructing highways undertaken in the form of the National Highway Development Project (NHDP), to be supplemented by initiatives for improving road connectivity in rural areas. Even in early 2008, the total length of expressways in the country was only two hundred kilometers, and four-lane national highways totaled about eight thousand kilometers in length. A major feature of financing NHDP in India was to move away from the usual practice of funding roads from general tax revenues, and instead to depend on a levy on fuel going into an earmarked Central Road Fund. Nearly two-thirds of the funding of NHDP projects was from the fuel levy. In China, financing depends more on tolls than on a fuel levy. There was also a change in Indian practice in moving to a system in which the operator has an incentive to ensure the quality of construction and proper maintenance over the entire duration of the contract. Although initially NHDP was implemented exclusively by a government authority mainly through civil works contracts, gradually it moved to a public-private partnership (P-P-P) mode so that all new projects are now expected to be undertaken in a build-operate-transfer (BOT) or equivalent mode. In view of the widespread resistance to tolls (and also their effects of economic distortions and traffic diversion, as have happened in China), the general presumption in India is that for BOT projects in the road sector, the government will provide a subsidy (of course, subject to its severe budget constraints) in the form of an annuity flow to meet the shortfall between anticipated revenue and loan repayment obligations, going for projects with the lowest bid for subsidy from prospective private investors. Although the private sector's share in the overall risk capital has so far been small in NHDP, the trend is toward a large-scale transfer of financing and traffic risk to the private sector. In China, private finance in road investments has been much less than 10 percent so far.

Railways

Growth in this sector in China has lagged behind other infrastructure sectors.[1] Operations are still highly centralized (unlike in highways and electricity, where there is more autonomy at the provincial and enterprise level) and not fully commercialized (the rate of return on investment in railways is lower than in other sectors)—see Bai and Qian (2008). Yet this sector's performance in China is much better in most respects than in India. Extension of railway network and throughput capacity in China has exceeded that in India. Average output per employee in China is more than twice that in India. In freight the daily output per wagon operated is four times that in India. Maintenance of assets is much better in China. The Ministry of Railways in China has entered into management contracts with the fourteen Regional Railway Administrations, with closely monitored competition and management incentives. The major restructuring that China Railways has undergone since the late 1990s toward commercial orientation has not yet happened in India, particularly in the bulk of its operations. In spite of some improvements in profitability in recent years, the Indian Railways remains an overmanned, decrepit behemoth, with a large backlog of overdue equipment and track replacement, maintenance, and safety enhancement. Staff costs account for more than half of working expenses in Indian Railways (but only a quarter in China). Average freight tariff per ton-kilometer in India is more than 60 percent above that in China (though containerization of freight traffic has been faster in India). China has largely eliminated the cross-subsidy from freight traffic to passenger traffic, whereas it is still substantial in India. In general, China Railways is less encumbered than Indian Railways with unprofitable public service obligations and employment generation demands, its investments (for example, in a great number of new lines) are less politicized, and railway management is granted more autonomy. Over the years Indian populist politics has wreaked havoc on commercial operations and investments in this sector.

[1] In the major stimulus spending since late 2008, government investment in railways, particularly in the interior areas, has been emphasized.

III

We shall now briefly discuss urban infrastructure, ports, and tele-communications. In urban infrastructure, India is all too visibly ill-equipped to cope with the already mounting demands arising from urban growth. Chinese investment in this area has been much larger than Indian investment. For example, even by 2002 (before the pre-Olympic hectic building activities started) capital investment in infrastructure in Beijing was nearly fourteen times that in Mumbai. In China, urban infrastructure is constructed, operated, and main-tained by separate companies set up by the city government (with a larger stake in cost recovery), whereas in India the municipal government itself performs these functions through its own depart-ments. The latter are financially strapped, as they do not have much taxation or borrowing power and are perpetually dependent on the state government for funds. In general, the fiscal system is much more decentralized in China. The share of municipal revenue as a proportion of total (state and central) government revenue in India was only about 2.3 percent in 2001–2002. Cost recovery from user charges for municipal services is less than one-fourth of the expen-diture incurred by the municipal bodies. The average investment re-quirement for urban infrastructure, including basic civic amenities, mass urban transportation, and road infrastructure, is estimated to be several times the revenue income of these municipal bodies.[2]

In India it is not just a matter of the fiscal system not being decentralized enough. Mayors in some cities do not have enough executive power or accountability to the local citizenry. It has been remarked in connection with the much better handling of mon-soon flooding by the Chennai municipal government than by the Mumbai government that the political setups in the two cities are remarkably different, with the city administration more accountable to the local people in Chennai. On a related matter, Ren and Wein-

---

[2] These numbers are from a 2008 study of municipal finances by the Development Re-search Group of the Reserve Bank of India, with data from thirty-five metropolitan municipal corporations.

stein (2008) compare the progress of two recent large-scale development projects in Shanghai and Mumbai (though their objectives are not quite comparable). In 2002, after Shanghai won the bid to host the 2010 World Expo, the city government quickly designated prime land along the Huangpu River in the central city, and in less than two years acquired the necessary land and relocated thousands of residents and dozens of factories, warehouses, and shipyards. In Mumbai, the Dharavi Redevelopment Project has been in the works since 1997, and it has taken more than ten years just to negotiate with the different contending parties involved on a proposal, not for relocation, but for on-site "rehabilitation" of most of Dharavi's residents and many commercial activities, and to convince the state government to allocate the political and financial resources required for the project. Although the democratic polity of India inevitably and justifiably requires such laborious political consensus building,[3] to which the Chinese government gives short shrift, it is also a fact, as Ren and Weinstein emphasize, that the Shanghai municipal government has much more autonomy and resource flexibility to carry out fast-track megaprojects that are completely lacking in Mumbai.

It is, of course, also a question of local resources. The antiquated (and corrupt) property tax systems in Indian cities prevent city finance from adequately benefiting from the ongoing real estate boom. In Indian cities there is no fund like the Urban Maintenance and Construction Fund in China (of which, in 2002, 19 percent came from funds raised by the urban utility company, 28 percent from domestic loans with government guarantees, and 10 percent from an earmarked urban maintenance and construction tax). User charges in India for water, sewage, and solid waste disposal services are kept abysmally low under political pressure. Metering is not widespread, and billing and enforcement of payment often perfunctory. It is not a coincidence that while Beijing has twenty-four-hour water service, residents of Delhi or Mumbai can expect only four to five hours of

[3] Of course, as many activists would be quick to point out, large numbers of people are still dissatisfied with the authorities in the Dharavi Redevelopment Project, and there are many outstanding issues of displacement yet to be resolved.

service per day on average. There is some hope that the National Urban Renewal Mission launched at the end of 2005 by the central government will over time make the provision of basic urban services financially more sustainable in India, and also strengthen local self-governance.

With the dramatic growth in output and exports from China's coastal cities, there has been a corresponding fast-paced development in port facilities. Shanghai and Shenzen have become the world's leading container ports after Hong Kong and Singapore. The number of days in turnaround time for ships in Shanghai is a fraction of that in the Mumbai port. The preferred mode of ownership and management has been that of joint ventures with substantial foreign investment, also moving from highly centralized control to decentralized management. Port authorities were either created for or transferred to municipal bodies as well as endowed with financial autonomy in the routine administration and operation of ports. The main sources of finance, apart from foreign investments mainly by Hong Kong- or Singapore-based terminal-operating multinational companies, are nongovernment investments and port construction fees.

In India there has been some significant improvement in the principal indicators of port efficiency at the major ports, often induced by inter- and intraport competition in getting business, though those indicators still remain much below international best practice. The average turnaround time has declined from 8.1 days in 1990–1991 to 3.6 days in 2006–2007 (in the best ports in the world turnaround time is measured in hours, much less than a day). Only about 13 percent of India's port capacity handles container traffic. Private-sector participation in major ports has been mainly under licensing of operations of existing container berths or granting of build-own-operate-transfer (BOOT) concessions for increasing terminal capacity. Unlike in China, corporatization of the port authority has not advanced, largely on account of opposition from labor unions. So far, Indian port tariffs are generally higher than other ports, and Indian port efficiency, despite the improvements, compares poorly with the world's major ports, including those in the region, such as Colombo, Shanghai, and Singapore. In a World Bank study of overall logistics performance related to ease and affordability of arranging international shipments, India is ranked fortieth, compared to China's twenty-eighth and Hong Kong's seventh.

Telecommunications is one infrastructural sector in which India has almost matched the astonishing growth of China in recent years. In fact, India now even has a cost advantage over China in this sector. Of course, China's average teledensity is much better than India's, largely because of better spread in rural areas, and Indian cities are worse off in bandwidth adequacy. The private sector is much more vigorous in Indian telecommunications, whereas in China SOEs still dominate, although functions such as operations and regulation have been separated and entities have been given financial flexibility. Some commentators suggest that the dramatic progress in the Indian telecom sector shows the potential achievements of privatization in clearing India's staggering deficit in a whole range of other infrastructural facilities. Of course, much depends on how conducive the regulatory environment is to competition. One also should not overlook the special nature of telecom as a sector. Dramatic reductions in cost in recent years in this sector have allowed technological leap-frogging and retention of high profitability even with the spread of competition in a way that is not easily replicable in other sectors.

In the other infrastructural sectors, particularly in power, roads, and railways, political exigencies and pressures of electoral populism in India keep user charges low, even blowing the state budget in the process, hampering investment incentives, and perpetuating delays in separating government functions from commercial operations, a matter in which China has advanced much more. In addition in China the decentralization of public finance even at the subprovincial level and close collaboration between local business and local government officials have enabled much better funding and facilitation of local infrastructure projects than in India. Corruption associated with such projects, in the form of kickbacks and quality dilution, has been rampant in both countries (in spite of much harsher punishment of a few officials in China from time to time). In India, high levels of electoral turnover has often meant the beginning of some infrastructure projects but not their successful completion or sustained maintenance. Foundation stones once laid with elaborate ceremony and etched with the name of now forgotten politicians litter the countryside in splendid desolation. Political clientelism has also meant that Indian politicians often concentrate more on spending public money on distribution of small-scale, recurrent, private (or "club") goods to their selected beneficiaries than on investment in larger, long-term public goods, which benefit a larger population but have fewer immediate and identifiable political rewards. The voter as an individual citizen is also usually more vigilant about nondelivery of the former than the latter.

Politicization of decisions on user charges has also seriously undermined the independence of regulatory bodies in the infrastructural sector in India. The institution of public hearings held by regulators has largely become hollow. Consumers take their grievances about unpopular tariff rate decisions directly to the ruling politicians, who, more often than not, are quick to get them revoked, bypassing the regulators. When consumers do bring their case to the regulatory hearings, it is mostly a one-way process, without the regulators proactively engaging them in an interactive deliberative process, which would have given the regulators more legitimacy with consumers and other stakeholders and would have had the potential of leading to informed political compromises among all parties involved.

Chapter 5

High Saving, Low Financial Intermediation

By official accounts, both China and India are high savers (and investors) for their range of per capita income. As shown in tables 3 and 4, the domestic (gross) saving rate in 2005 was 42 percent in China and 31 percent in India (in 2008 they were even higher, 54 percent in China and 38 percent for India); the Chinese rate is, of course, the highest in the world, but even the Indian rate is higher[1] than that anywhere in the much richer countries of North and South America, for example. It has been suggested—see, for example, Heston (2008)—that, investment goods being relatively expensive in China and India by world standards, in international purchasing power parity terms the saving (and investment) rates in these two countries are overstated[2] in the official estimates in national currencies. Nevertheless, the rates remain high particularly for developing countries.

Let's look at the composition of these savings and investments. Both countries have depended primarily on domestic financing of their investments. In both countries, household savings form a major part of total domestic savings, though in recent years enterprise savings (business retained earnings) have outstripped household

---

[1] The average investment rate in India was about 34 percent in the period 2003–2004 to 2007–2008.

[2] For example, in PPP terms the Chinese investment rate has been estimated to be 32 percent in 2004.

TABLE 3
Saving and Investment in China (Percentage of GDP)

	1990	1995	2000	2005
Domestic saving	38.7	41.2	38.2	42.0
Households	20.0	20.0	16.4	16.0
Government	7.3	4.8	6.3	6.0
Enterprise	11.4	16.4	15.5	20.0
Investment	34.7	40.8	36.3	41.0
Household	6.4	2.7	5.5	6.0
Government	3.6	5.2	3.5	4.0
Enterprise	24.7	32.9	27.3	31.0
Current account (S−I)	4.0	0.4	1.9	1.0

Source: Kuijs (2005, 2006)

savings in importance in China. The household saving rate in China is high relative to rich countries, but lower than in India (India's savers earn a higher rate of return than the repressed rate in China). Households are net lenders to other sectors in both countries, largely through deposits in banks and post offices. The largest component of household investment in both countries is physical investment, much of it in the form of residential investment (and livestock in rural areas).

TABLE 4
Saving and Investment in India (Percentage of GDP)

	1990	1995	2000	2005
Domestic saving	21.8	24.4	24.8	31.1
Households	17	18.6	21.1	21.6
Government	2.4	2.3	−0.8	2.4
Enterprise	2.4	3.5	4.5	7.1
Investment*	23.7	23.5	25.3	28.4
Households	9.2	6.7	10.5	11.4
Government	10.2	9.3	7.4	7.1
Enterprise	4.4	7.5	7.4	9.9
Current account (S−I)	−1.9	0.9	−0.5	2.7

Source: Reserve Bank of India (2008).
Note* Investment = gross capital formation

Why are the household saving rates so high? A large part of it may be in the form of precautionary saving, as state- or employer-supported retirement and health benefits are scarce, particularly in the vast rural sector (and the urban informal sector) of both countries, and as the tradition of extended family with mutual support declines. In China the household saving rate has gone up substantially since the prereform days, when the social protection system (the "iron rice bowl") was still intact. The Chinese demographic transition, with the prospect of old-age support from children diminishing with the one-child policy and with the working age population relative to dependents going up fast in the past few decades, certainly helped saving; this effect will start declining as the demographics shift in the near future in China (and will rise in India as the earner-dependent ratio is expected to rise over the next few decades). Saving was also induced by the privatization of urban housing in China and the proliferation of investment opportunities after reforms started, particularly in self-financed enterprises (but ceilings on deposit interest rates remained a damper on general household saving). Consumption growth lagged behind the high rates of income growth, particularly in China; financial liabilities were low as credit constraints for households and small producers were severe in both countries. The situation is improving for the general population rather slowly. The spread of consumer durables (and mortgaged housing) and retail credit to finance them came to both countries only very recently. In both countries the spread of state-owned bank branches and post offices helped mobilize rural saving. In India after the nationalization of the large banks in 1969 and a determined policy of rural branch banking, household financial saving as a percentage of GDP multiplied almost six times in the twenty-five years after 1970. In China, rural household saving rates are much higher than the rates for urban households (possibly reflecting precautionary saving, as social protection is significantly better in the urban sector), and so, as Reidel, Jin, and Gao (2007) point out, the increasing rural-urban per capita income gap and population shift toward the urban sector may have put downward pressure on the household savings rate in China in recent years, outweighing the positive effect of rising per capita income in general; on the other hand, as the private burden of housing, education, and health care increases, even urban households need to save more.

Relatively high enterprise saving distinguishes China from the rest of the world. Enterprise saving mainly from retained earnings has emerged as the largest source of saving. Reasons for high saving by enterprises include a large share of capital-intensive industry (often state-owned) and low dividend policies (since access to the equity or bond market is limited). Enterprise investment is also one of the highest in the world. In the first half of the 1990s, the enterprise sector's net financing from outside (largely bank loans) was 40 to 50 percent; more recently it was about 30 percent. Alternative earnings from investing bank deposits are not attractive for enterprises, as the repressed deposit rate is much lower than the bank lending rate. In China investment in inventories used to be substantial (as was usual in centrally planned economies), but that has declined and now the bulk of investment is accounted for by gross fixed capital formation. There has been a major shift in ownership of fixed capital in China. In 1990, SOEs accounted for two-thirds of the fixed capital; by 2005, the situation has reversed itself: non-state-owned enterprises accounted for almost two-thirds of the fixed capital.

Enterprise saving and investment rates are much smaller in India than in China. The enterprise saving rate increased between 1990 and 2005; Mohan (2008) attributes this increase to three causes: a decline in corporate tax rates, a decline in the cost of debt servicing, and a rise in the ratio of retained earnings to profit after tax. India's enterprise sector is a net borrower, but to a much smaller extent than China's. Almost all of the investment in India is in fixed capital and the share of inventory investment is minimal.

The official data suggest that there has been a large jump in investment by the private corporate sector in India, from nearly 20 percent of total fixed investment in 1990 to about 40 percent in the years around 2005. There are reasons[3] to believe that this estimate

---

[3] For a spelling out of these reasons, see Nagaraj (2008). As noted in footnote 6 in chapter 2, the report of the National Statistical Commission (2001) also raises doubts about the methods of estimating the official private corporate-sector investment.

of a large increase is not reliable. Since the private corporate sector accounts for less than 10 percent of GDP, it is hard to believe that this sector could account for the fastest-growing part of domestic saving and the largest segment of domestic investment. This also suggests that the usual claim that the private corporate sector has been the main engine of the recent growth in India has to be qualified somewhat. (For some questions on the Indian growth data, see the appendix to chapter 2.)

In 2005, the government saving rate in China was 6 percent of GDP, which is high compared to most countries. High government saving has been the result of a growth-oriented economic policy emphasizing investment. Government consumption in China is relatively low. Although there is little difference in direct government investment with other countries, large capital transfers to SOEs (around 5 percent of GDP) distinguish China from most other countries.

Government saving in India is low compared to China. The government saving rate in India averaged around 3 percent till the 1980s. In the 1990s, however, the government saving rate began to fall, with a decline in the tax-GDP ratio, largely caused by the initial effects of tax reform and the decline in customs revenue with trade reform. In terms of tax-GDP ratio, India is undertaxed compared to China. Meanwhile, revenue expenditure (salaries, subsidies, etc.) and interest outlays on the large public debt (much larger than in China) continued to rise. In view of the deteriorating health of public-sector finances, the Fiscal Responsibility and Budget Management (FRBM) Act was passed in 2003. Following the introduction of the FRBM Act at the central level and fiscal responsibility laws at the state level, and the reform/rationalization of the tax system (decline in tax rates, expansion of tax base, increased access to service taxes, and improved tax administration), some expenditure control, and turnaround in some public enterprises, public-sector saving went up. The government saving rate turned positive in 2004 and was 2.4 percent in 2005. But in the years since then, the large increase in subsidies (food, fertilizers, petroleum products, etc.) and other populist programs (agricultural loan waiver, salary raises for government employees,[4] etc.) put pressure on government saving (with the fiscal deficit rising to about 10 percent of GDP in 2008–2009).[5] This tends to dry up liquidity in the system, which affects the cost of capital, and the ax often falls on productive government expenditures. The government investment rate has declined since 1990, with adverse consequences for sectors such as infrastructure, both rural and urban, as discussed in chapters 3 and 4.

II

In both China and India the financial system is dominated by banks, and the banks are largely state-controlled. As table 5 shows, bank deposits and currency form the largest portion of financial assets in both countries, particularly in China[6] (equity and government debt are more important in India than in China).

In India 90 percent of the assets of pension funds and 50 percent of life insurance assets are required to be held in government bonds and related securities; this degree of risk aversion is one major reason why demand for corporate bonds and equities is lower than in rich countries.

State-controlled banks have about 85 percent of banking business as measured by share of deposits. Indian banks lend only 60 percent of their deposits, compared to 130 percent for Chinese banks. Of the total bank credit in India in 2005, 39 percent went to public-sector enterprises, 30 percent to corporate discretionary lending, 11 percent to agriculture, 7 percent to household enterprises and proprietorships, and 13 percent to small private companies. The last three categories fall under what in India is called "priority sector," where there is perceived to be underlending in relation to social

---

[4] The large majority of government employees, usually in the lower echelons, earn salaries much above their opportunity income in the private sector, for the same qualifications.

[5] Since then the global recession has brought about forces that will only raise the fiscal deficit to GDP ratio.

[6] With increased tax benefits for long-term bank deposits, the ratio of bank deposits to total financial assets in India has gone up in recent years.

TABLE 5
Financial Assets as Percentage of GDP in China and India, 2004

	China	India
Equity	32	56
Corporate debt	11	2
Government debt	17	34
Bank deposits/currency	160	68
Total	220	160

Source: McKinsey Quarterly (August 2006)

returns to credit. One of the objectives of nationalization of major banks and general regulations of all banking was to help these particularly credit-constrained areas of the economy, even though the loans were often unprofitable. Banerjee, Cole, and Duflo (2004) examine the evidence on bank performance in India and arrive at the following conclusions, among others:

(a) There is substantial underlending in India, but bank ownership seems to have had a limited impact on the government's ability to direct credit to specific underserved sectors. Up to the early 1990s the government set interest rates and required both public and private banks to issue 40 percent of credit to the priority sector and to meet specific subtargets within the priority sector. Compared to private banks, public banks provided substantially more credit to agriculture, rural areas, and the government, at the expense of credit to trade, transportation, and finance. Of course, private banks did not feel the same political pressure as public banks to lend (sometimes imprudently) to the politically important rural clientele. But there was not much difference between private and public banks in credit to small-scale industry. Since the 1990s, the private banks have been more dynamic in terms of credit, deposits, and number of branches opened, including in rural areas. Bank interest rates were mostly deregulated by the end of the 1990s.

(b) The main reason why the public banks have not substantially solved the underlending problem is that the official lending rules are rigid, and on top of that the public loan officers do not use whatever little flexibility they have, largely because of the incentives and constraints they face. Their rewards are at best weakly tied to their success in making imaginative lending decisions; on the other hand, failed loans can lead to investigations for possible fraud by the Central Vigilance Commission. So instead of being aggressive in lending, they often take the safer route of parking the money in government bonds. One should, however, add that private banks also come to have more bureaucratic rules when they are consolidated and become larger: the chain of control becomes longer and more rigid lending rules replace discretion of the local loan officers. Thus, much depends on the internal managerial reforms in the banks, both private and public.

Of course, competition from private and foreign banks has driven many changes in the banking sector as a whole. Increased competition and greater autonomy have resulted in public-sector banks focusing more on profitability. Public-sector banks increased the ratio of their net profits to assets from 0.57 percent in 1997 to 0.82 percent in 2006, in line with the profitability of the new private banks. But the overstaffing of public banks, compared to private banks, continues; the amount of total deposits per employee is nearly twice as much in private banks as in public banks. This contributes to the fact that India has one of the highest costs of financial intermediation in the world. India's private-sector companies pay interest rates that are, on average, nearly twice as high as the rates their Chinese counterparts pay.

An important area of recent reforms has been in improving prudential norms related to capital adequacy and asset classification. The Board of Financial Supervision introduced regulatory norms that were in line with international best practices with regard to income recognition, asset classification, reporting, and loan provisioning. Work to introduce the new Basel II Accord (which sets international standards for bank capital reserve requirements) is under way. The adoption of Basel norms has improved the capital adequacy of banks substantially. By 2006, the situation with nonperforming assets (NPAs) of Indian banks was no different from that of major banks in foreign countries and the difference between the private and public banks on NPAs was eliminated (although the NPA situation may have worsened in the last year or so with the large rural loan waiver program).

In 2002, bankruptcy laws were revamped to improve the recovery of debts. The new Secured Lending Law allowed banks to recover the assets that had been used to secure loans in the event of nonpayment of interest or capital.

In the prereform period public-sector banks and the Reserve Bank of India (RBI) served as a vehicle for monetization of government deficits. At the beginning of the reforms, banks were required to lend 63.5 percent of their assets to the government in the form of the statutory liquidity ratio (SLR) and the cash reserve ratio (CRR). By April 2003, such preemptions were reduced to less than 30 percent. The RBI can now alter these ratios depending on prevailing economic and monetary conditions. As of August 2008, the CRR ratio was 8.75 percent and the SLR was 25 percent. Following the FRBM Act in 2003, the RBI ceased to participate in the primary market for government securities and no longer lends to the government.

As mentioned earlier, in China the banking sector is more dominant in the financial system and state control even more pervasive than in India (in 2004, in China the state owned 83 percent of total bank assets; in India it was 75 percent). Most bank lending in China is concentrated among four large[7] state-owned commercial banks (SOCB), which are closely supervised and controlled by the central bank. Most of the loans are directed to SOEs, and the private sector accounts for less than one-third of the loans, far below the share in most developing countries.[8] The banks are often run by politicians and bureaucrats rather than by banking professionals. The biggest weakness of the Chinese banking system is its share of nonperforming loans (NPL). According to official statistics, the ratio of NPLs

---

[7] The assets of the largest of these four banks exceed the total value of all financial assets in India.

[8] Using a World Bank dataset from World Business Environment Survey, Huang (2006) finds that domestic private firms in China report substantially more serious financing constraints than their counterparts in India, even after a number of firm- and industry-level characteristics are controlled for.

to GDP was as high as 22.5 percent in 2000 and has declined to 7.3 percent in 2005,[9] which is much larger than the ratio in India. Some independent analysts argue that the official statistics underestimate the extent of NPLs. First, the official figures on NPLs do not include the bad loans that have been transferred from banks to state-owned asset management companies. If one adds these bad loans to the official NPL numbers, the total amount of NPLs increases by two-thirds. Second, the classification of the NPLs has been problematic in China. The Basel Committee on Banking Supervision classifies a loan as "doubtful" or "bad" when any interest payment is overdue by 180 days. In China, this step is not taken until the principal payment is delayed beyond the loan maturity date and in many cases until the borrower declares bankruptcy.

After the large injection of fresh capital in the SOCBs, beginning in 2003, the profitability of the banking sector as a whole improved by 2004. Nonetheless, the profitability of Chinese banks continues to be below international standards. In any case many of the underlying causes of nonperforming loans (in terms of managerial practices and incentives) have remained the same. The large banks continue to lend to many of the same clients whose loans were written off in the earlier bank recapitalizations. Pressure to give out more loans has increased in the current downturn and with the stimulus program. There is ample evidence that businesses owned by Communist Party members are significantly more likely to get loans from the banks. In addition to the SOCBs, the authorities are facing the task of resolving substantial financial problems in other key segments, notably the rural commercial banks, whose NPLs were 23 percent of their total loans at the end of 2004.

Competition in the banking sector has risen markedly as the SOCBs have moved away from their traditional specialization and as joint-stock banks (JSBs) have developed. There has been a moderate decline in the SOCB share of commercial bank assets, from 76 percent of depository institution loans to nonfinancial sectors in

---

[9] As Chinese banks are now being urged by the government to lend more vigorously under the stimulus program in the current economic downturn, the NPL ratio is likely to go up significantly.

1998 to just under 60 percent of the total in 2004. The largest part of this reduction is due to the growth in assets of the JSBs, whose share of loans more than doubled during that period. The growth of the JSB segment has improved the overall competitiveness of the banking sector in recent years, but its impact on allocative efficiency of capital is not yet clear. Also, although permitted nationwide scope in their operations, most of the JSBs have a heavy focus on coastal provinces and, with the exception of a few, have much more limited presence in interior provinces. Despite the entry of foreign banks, the level and the scope of foreign bank activities in China remains small.

In 2004 the central bank decided to remove the ceiling on bank lending rates. Nonetheless, interest rates are heavily influenced by the rate set by the central bank on excess reserves. Moreover, the dominance of the SOCBs in the bond market limits the liquidity in the market.

III

India has had an equity market for a long time, but it was very thin and fragmented. The Bombay Stock Exchange (BSE), the largest of the stock exchanges, was a closed market, acting mainly in the interest of its members. The 1990s saw many reforms in the equity market, particularly increasing competition, participation, and liquidity, improving transparency in the price discovery mechanism, improving regulation and supervision in general, and reducing the settlement period. The setting up of the Securities and Exchange Board of India (SEBI) in 1992 as an independent regulator marked a break from the previous regulatory regime. It played a major role in improving transparency and competition, though delays in the legal system often hindered the process. In 1994 a new National Stock Exchange (NSE) was created with a corporate structure and a professional team managing the operations (rather than a body of brokers). It rapidly became the largest stock market in India and the third largest in the world, measured by the number of transactions.

The establishment of the NSE and some innovations in trading information systems had a significant impact on both trading costs and liquidity in the equity market. Private-sector companies account for about 70 percent of market capitalization.

In China, the equity markets play a much more limited role than the banking system in providing financing, they are highly speculative, and they are often driven by insider trading. The two domestic stock exchanges were established in 1990. At the end of 2005, the market capitalization of China's stock exchanges was ranked fifteenth in the world, with a significant fraction of shares not traded. The listing of shares is subject to the approval of the China Securities Regulatory Commission (CSRC), which gives priority to SOEs;[10] 80 percent of the listed companies are under government control. Financial institutions have relatively restricted access to the market. In recent years the government has taken some measures to improve the functioning of the stock market, including giving more access to smaller companies and making the decisions on listing companies more transparent. As long as the government, which is the primary participant in the stock market, continues also to be the regulator, however, the prospects of improving the efficiency of the Chinese stock markets will remain limited.

In comparison to the equity markets, the reforms in the Indian bond market have been slow. The large presence of the government as both an owner and regulator distorts incentives for reform. In spite of some improvements, the bond market suffers from lack of liquidity and poor participation. The corporate bond market is regulated by SEBI. This market is very small, with total outstanding corporate bonds being equal to 1.5 percent of GDP in 2005. Onerous documentation requirements have resulted in an almost complete absence of traded corporate bonds. In recent years companies have increased their reliance on external commercial borrowing, but the international financial crisis has underlined the dangers involved in such reliance.

[10] The composition of SEBI in India is more professional than CSRC in China; the latter is often full of political appointees.

Cumbersome regulations also characterize China's corporate bond market, which is also underdeveloped. Outstanding issues are less than 1 percent of GDP, making it the smallest market in relative terms in Asia. In other segments of the bond market domination by the government is pervasive. In any case the bond market is a very small part of the financial system in China.

Overall, these are two high-saving countries, with China having a much larger financial pool to draw on. But in China the state-controlled large banks dominate the whole financial system, paying their depositors a below-market rate, nonperforming loans remain a significant burden, and allocation of capital remains severely distorted, particularly working against private enterprise, which accounts now for more than half of GDP and against rural producers, particularly in the interior provinces. India's financial system is somewhat more balanced than China's in terms of banking, equity, and bond markets as sources of formal finance. It is also better regulated and less saddled with bad loans, but the banking sector still ignores a large part of the economy, with small enterprises seriously underserved. With high government borrowing, the cost of capital in the Indian economy remains high. In both countries the informal sector remains the major (though sometimes more expensive or short-term) source of finance for most ordinary people and small businesses; India's larger informal sector is reflected in the fact that India's informal lending market is much larger than China's. But even China's smaller informal sector (often illegal) has been influential; as Tsai (2007) points out, certain curb market innovations have already contributed to liberalizing the formal financial system. As the public sector with its guaranteed social protection declines in both countries, demand for new financial products and services will increase.[11]

---

[11] In India, for example, the share of life insurance in total household financial assets climbed to 18 percent in 2008.

Chapter 6

The Pattern of Burgeoning Capitalism

In both countries, some form of weak capitalism had developed many decades before Liberation or Independence. After Liberation, China installed a socialist economy both in industry and (beginning in the mid-1950s) agriculture; the private sector was minimal and operated on a minute scale and in the shadows. For the first four decades after Independence, India had a much larger private sector than China did, but many of India's key and strategic industries were in the public sector, sometimes coexisting with the private sector in the same industry (for example, steel) and in other cases without private-sector competition (for example, power-plant equipment manufacturing or airlines). In the last two decades the private corporate sector has thrived in India, even though in the formal sector state-owned companies still account for about 40 per cent of total sales. The Indian informal sector (including both farms and household enterprises outside agriculture), much larger than that in China, has been mostly privately owned; even now it employs nearly 94 percent of the labor force. But many of these tiny enterprises, often family owned, cannot quite be described as capitalist business; if market prices are imputed for the inputs they use (such as family labor) their business income is often persistently negative. They operate in the interstices of a low-productivity "involuted" economy, the capitalist parts of which cannot absorb them.

Given the ideology of the long-ruling Communist Party, the transition to capitalism in China is the more fascinating, and still somewhat contested, story. Most people will agree that while the Party retains its monopoly on power, much of the economy is no longer a "command economy," with the market mechanism now being the major allocator of resources. About 95 percent of consumer prices are now market determined, though the state still controls prices in some key sectors such as financial services, telecommunications, utilities, and energy. But is the economy primarily capitalist now, with private owners of capital providing the dominant mode of organizing social and economic life through their drive for profit-making and accumulation? The answer is still ambiguous, but there are some telling straws in the wind.

First, quantitatively how important is private ownership now? It is not easy to classify Chinese firms by their ownership or to distinguish between private control rights and other forms of public or semipublic control rights or to trace their varying shares in a firm.[1] One can only make rough guesses. In a dataset compiled by the National Bureau of Statistics for very large industrial firms (more than five million yuan in sales), a 2005 report by the Organisation for Economic Co-operation and Development (OECD) finds that there are different categories of shareholders in the firms: state (direct or indirect), collective (controlled by local governments), individuals, "domestic legal persons," and foreign companies (when foreign share capital exceeds 50 percent in a company). Assuming that the last three categories constitute private ownership, the OECD report concludes from the data that the private sector contributed 52.3 percent of the industrial value added in 2003.[2] But this has been challenged by Huang (2008), who suggests that much of the "legal person" share of capital originates in the state sector (when SOEs hold significant equity stakes in other firms). Although excluding the "legal person" category will reduce the private-sector share, it is most likely that the OECD estimate is an underestimate of the private sector's contribution to the overall industrial value

[1] Huang (2008) shows how convoluted the ownership structure is even in China's most successful private-sector firm, Huawei Technology Corporation.

[2] An alternative estimate by Perkins and Rawski (2008) puts private ownership (domestic and foreign) as contributing 52 percent of industrial output in 2005.

added,[3] as the nonlarge firms not included in this dataset are more likely to have a larger percentage of private ownership. In the rest of the economy, particularly in agriculture, retail and wholesale trade, and the informal service sector, private ownership rights (or at least control rights) predominate. So altogether, the Chinese economy is primarily privately owned or controlled today.

But even over the past two decades, the evolution of the private sector to reach its current position has been tortuous and elusive. As late as 1988, private firms with more than eight employees were not permitted. Many private firms operated below the radar and used various subterfuges and covert deals with local officials, as they prospered and adapted themselves to the changing permissible mores. Some of them used to be called "red-hat capitalists," sometimes hiding under the façade of local collectives. Only since the late 1990s have they slowly taken off their red hats and started coming out of the closet. For many years government policy discriminated against domestic private capital in matters of finance, market access, and regulatory approvals. As the profitability of TVEs declined with more intense competition, the fiscal gains relative to the responsibilities from hanging on to them diminished for local governments. This, along with collusion between local officials and local business, led to the policy of *fang xiao* ("let go the small") and privatization of TVEs. Legal status of (particularly urban) private companies and their access to bank finance slowly improved over the 1990s, especially after the official recognition of their importance at the Fifteenth Party Congress in 1997. Foreign investment was in joint ventures with SOEs in the 1980s, but has mostly gone to wholly owned or joint-venture private companies since the mid-1990s. More recently, business people were allowed to become members of the Communist Party, and already by 2005 there were more than ten million such members. Currently about one-third of the private entrepreneurs are members of the Party (including *xiahai*, entrepreneurs who are former officials).

[3] On the other hand, the share of the private sector in total fixed-asset investment is still relatively low. For a discussion, see Haggard and Huang (2008).

But the relationship between private business and the state is often rather clientelistic. Businesses provide support to the state leadership, accept its pervasive control and guidance, and are more interested in a predictable business environment than in full democratization of the polity, and in exchange they get political legitimacy and protection, better access to state resources, and at the local level even partnership with officials. The role of the municipal governments of Taizhou and Wenzhou of Zhejiang province in developing the private sector ahead of the full legalization of private property rights is among the best known. On the basis of a statistical analysis of a large and representative sample of private firms, Li et al. (2008) conclude that Party membership helps private entrepreneurs to obtain loans, to have more confidence in the operation of the legal system, and in general to improve firm performance. Of course, it is well known that some of the entrepreneurs are in fact friends or relatives of Party officials.[4] Many SOE's are controlled by powerful political families. Thus there is a new political-managerial class, the members of which over the past two decades have converted their positions of authority into wealth and power. The vibrancy of entre-preneurial ambitions combined with the arbitrariness of power in an authoritarian state has sometimes given rise to particularly corrupt or predatory forms of capitalism, unencumbered by the restraints of civil society institutions.[5]

Although the state has relaxed its earlier control over prices and allows markets and profit-making to be the major organizing principle of economic life, the state still dominates the producer-goods sectors, transportation, and finance. Although many of the state companies remain inert and inefficient behemoths, dependent on

[4] It was reported in *Der Spiegel*, February 27, 2007, that a study by the State Council of the Academy of Social Sciences and the Party's Central University found that of the 3,320 Chinese citizens with personal wealth of one hundred million yuan or more, about 2,932 were children of high-ranking Party officials.

[5] Perhaps nowhere has it been as starkly evident as in the real estate boom in cities where the commercial developers in cahoots with local officials have bulldozed old neighborhoods, with residents waking up in the morning to find that their houses have been marked for demolition with the Chinese character *chai* (meaning "raze") painted in white, with hardly any redress (or adequate compensation) available.

state largesse, though substantially leaner (and more commercialized) than before, some of them are now important players in the global market competition. Some of these companies are now market leaders in technology, cost control, design, and marketing—the areas of traditional weakness of SOEs. SOEs such as Chery Automobile (the majority shareholder of which is the municipal government of Wuhu), Baosteel, Chinalco, and Shanghai Electric have become market leaders in their respective arenas in the domestic market, outcompeting some reputed foreign companies.[6] Generally, in recruiting professional managers, broadening their investor base, and shedding their traditional social and political obligations, many SOEs do not conform to the usual stereotypes. While the private sector has created more jobs and absorbed many of the workers laid off by SOEs, the state still controls the larger and often more profitable (high-margin, more monopolistic) companies in the industrial and service sectors. The state's role in regulating the private sector also goes far beyond the usual functions in other countries—in bargaining the terms of foreign investment, negotiating the border prices of imported materials, channeling finance and investment to favored sectors, directing consolidation and merger of firms, and promoting industrial capabilities across sectors and regions. There are many cases where, even though the ownership rights are in the private sector, some part of the effective control rights over assets may still be directly or indirectly in the hands of the state. Recently during the global financial crisis, SOE's flush with loans from state banks, have taken over some small and medium size private enterprises that were struggling because of lack of finance. As a senior Chinese banker commented (quoted in the *Financial Times*, August 24, 2009), "It's quite hard to compete when you're playing against the referee."

An important question arises in the cases where an enterprise is managed on essentially commercial principles but the state, say at the local level, still owns or has control rights over a large share of the assets: is this a capitalist enterprise? Some may describe it as

[6] See "China's Champions," *Financial Times*, March 16, 2008.

capitalist if it follows the principle of shareholder value maximiza-tion. Others may point out that as long as substantial control rights remain with the state, which is subject to potentially arbitrary politi-cal influence, the internal dynamic logic of capitalism is missing. In late 2008, when China's richest man, Huang Guangyu was arrested, many thought his biggest crime was that he was getting too powerful for the political leadership's comfort (shades of Putin's Russia). (At the local level, even when career promotion prospects for Chinese local officials are linked to local growth objectives, other objectives, such as maintaining social stability, are in play and are subject to malleable objectives of the central Party leadership, which need not always be consistent with maximizing economic value.) The actual situation is, of course, even more fluid, as there are different degrees of state control rights, and with recent changes in stock ownership laws markets have become more liquid, loosening the control of state authorities over companies.

In general it is probably correct to say that while the Party can undo individual capitalists at short notice, it will be much more dif-ficult for the leadership to undo a whole network of capitalist rela-tions, by now thickly overlaid with vested interests of various kinds. Individual entrepreneurs may have a clientelistic relationship with the state, but the state, for all its relative autonomy, is now suffi-ciently enmeshed in a profit-oriented system that has been identified with legitimacy-enhancing international economic prowess and na-tionalist glory, a tiger that the political leadership may find difficult to dismount.

II

Some analysts find in China elements of the "developmental state," a familiar idea from the earlier East Asian growth literature. The role of large state-owned banks, including the China Development Bank (like the Korea Development Bank, Japan Development Bank, Taiwan Strategic Industry Fund, or the Small and Medium Business Guarantee Fund working in collaboration with the Taiwan Industrial

Development Bureau, in the rest of East Asia) has been crucial in industrial finance. In general the financial system has been at the service of a state-directed industrial policy. Successful private companies in China such as Huawei and Lenovo have benefited a great deal from their close ties with the government. As in the rest of East Asia, export promotion combined with domestic technological capacity building and state encouragement of trial and experimentation in exploring dynamic comparative advantage sometimes at the expense of static allocation efficiency have been at the core of the development strategy. Yet the Chinese case is also qualitatively different from the standard East Asian "developmental state" in several respects.

First, because of a different history of evolution of the private sector, which grew in the interstices of market reform in a socialist economy, the nature of "embeddedness" of the developmental bureaucracy[7] was quite different. As mentioned earlier, until quite recently private business operated below the radar, trying to insure against the vagueness and uncertainty of property rights by clustering with other private businesses in horizontal ties and building covert bridges with local government officials, and trying to overcome discrimination in access to state finance by drawing on lineage networks and overseas Chinese connections for credit and marketing. Thus, if Japan and South Korea are examples of "coordinated capitalism," in which the nation-state presided over and encouraged the coordination (of decisions and expectations) among private business conglomerates, the Chinese case has been described as that of state-led and -controlled development *from above*, and that of network or *guanxi* capitalism[8] *from below*, with a large number of small family-based businesses in the latter forming clusters with informal credit and trade links among themselves and with the diaspora, and often in tacit or even open cooperation with local officials. Taiwan also developed many clusters of business groups based on *guanxi* ties. The state in Taiwan initially (under Kuomintang leadership) had a

[7] See Evans (1995) for a discussion of the embeddedness of the East Asian bureaucracy in its close relations with private business.
[8] See McNally (2007).

weak connection with indigenous business, but over time it became much more active in promoting and financing private business than the government in mainland China.

Second, the issue of collaboration of private business with local officials also points to the substantial regional variations in the development of Chinese capitalism, as is inevitable in such a large country. Unlike in much of East Asia, fiscal and general economic decentralization has been more advanced in China, and that itself has led to a more diverse and diffuse industrial policy in operation, with a great deal of regional variance in industrial capability, business practices, and economic performance and also in the nature of state-business relationships. Intense competition between the enterprises of different localities and the strong link of cadre evaluation in the Party with local economic performance paved the way for local alliances between politicians and business managers, particularly in coastal China. But in some interior regions, competition as well as the pattern of this alliance was patchy, and in general local autonomy sometimes interfered with the implementation of a coordinated industrial policy in the country as a whole.

Third, FDI has played a much more important role in China, compared to South Korea, Taiwan, or Japan, in technological and managerial upgrading and international marketing. (In 2002, in ten large manufacturing subsectors in China at the two-digit level, foreign-invested firms accounted for nearly half of total sales.)[9] This is not unrelated to the weaker development of large private business in China.

The Indian case has also been quite different from the East Asian developmental state. Although private business firms have a long history in India, in the first three decades after Independence they were relatively subdued, largely played a subsidiary role to the state leadership and privileged state production in the strategic and heavy industries, and learned to work out niches and modes of operation in a heavily regulated industrial environment. The bureaucratic elite was not particularly probusiness, either by inclination or ideology,

[9] See Brandt, Rawski, and Sutton (2008), table 15.1.

or in terms of social composition (as the predominantly upper-caste officers often looked down on members of the mercantile castes), and did not have much of a direct stake in the fortunes of private capital. Of course, over time a well-oiled machinery of delivery of requisite permits and licenses in exchange for bribes and political funding for elections developed between large private business and the political class. The social composition of the bureaucratic and political leadership also changed over time, with increasingly active participation of business, trader and farmer families, and other caste groups in politics and administration. In some regions (particularly western and southern India) local connections between the upcoming new capitalists (many of them from agricultural castes) and political organizations and authorities flourished—as in the case of the Kammas in Andhra Pradesh, Patidars in Gujarat, the Marathas in the sugar cooperatives of Maharashtra, the Gounders and Nadars in Tamil Nadu, and so on. By the 1980s, both in terms of social transformation and increasing acceptability of the ideology of the marketplace and of private ownership, the political culture became increasingly market-friendly, though there was obvious reluctance on the part of officials to let go of their discretionary powers and powers of intervention. In any case, the tightly knit links between business and officialdom of the East Asian type were difficult to forge in India, where elite fragmentation in an extremely heterogeneous society and the exigencies of populist electoral politics make such tight links politically suspect.

Yet compared to the past, in the past couple of decades the link between the political or bureaucratic leadership and business associations (such as the Confederation of Indian Industry) on the matter of economic reform has been important in pushing the market principle and in slowly establishing the general hegemony of capital in the political culture. Some of the new entrepreneurs, belonging as they sometimes do to the families of bureaucrats, army officers, and other members of the professional classes or sharing ties through education in elite engineering and business schools, have forged new links between the bureaucracy and private capital. The incidence of such linkage has been stronger in some industries and regions than in others.

Pinglé (1999) shows that in recent years in some industries (for example, in computer software) bureaucrats have even acted as policy entrepreneurs and worked closely with private business with a kind of shared understanding and using informal channels of communication to achieve the goal of fostering private entrepreneurship. In some cases, strong intrabureaucratic ties and cohesion have enabled the policy entrepreneurs to withstand interventionist political pressure. This has not, however, been the case in India's steel industry. The private-sector steel company TISCO used to nimbly work its way through the restrictions of the erstwhile licensing regime and enjoy the monopoly rent they generated. The managers of the public-sector Steel Authority of India Ltd. (SAIL) were, however, hemmed in above by the interventionist Indian Administrative Service (IAS) bureaucrats in the Ministry of Steel and below by the contentious labor unions, which were historically associated with politicians. In contrast, the state-owned automobile firm Maruti Udyog Ltd. (MUL) was managed better, largely due to better channels of communication and a nonhierarchical relationship between the IAS bureaucrats and senior MUL management. The alliance between managers and bureaucrats allowed it to innovate in the matter of corporate strategy and industrial relations, in particular to handle intransigent unions more effectively than in the steel industry. In the labor-repressive regime of the East Asian developmental state the business-bureaucracy alliance had to worry much less about methods of maintaining good industrial relations than in the active adversarial setup of a fractious and fragmented union movement that characterizes the Indian labor scene. In the computer software industry or other IT industries, handling trade unions was in any case less of a problem, and in addition, as is common in a new industry at the technological frontier, there was some entente between the technocrats at specialized government departments such as the Department of Electronics or the Department of Information Technology and the private entrepreneurs (and their compact business associations such as NASSCOM), often sharing similar backgrounds and professional qualifications.

At the state government level there has been a similar entente between regional capital and the state administration, at least in some states (for example, Gujarat, Andhra Pradesh, and Tamil Nadu). Sinha (2005) emphasizes the strategies that regional elites and politicians have played all along in navigating through (and mitigating) even the prereform restrictive policy regime of the central government at its local implementation level, in their pursuit of the regional developmental state (as in Gujarat). Even in the domain legally under the control of the central Ministry of Industry, the porous nature of the structure of joint industrial governance leaves enough room for regional elites to maneuver. The regional political imperatives were, of course, different in different parts of India and, accordingly, the institutional practices and outcomes were sharply different, as the contrasting cases of Gujarat and West Bengal show. Even after the major deregulatory reforms since the mid-80's, the state governments hold considerable power over a new firm (in getting land, water and electricity connections and labor and environmental clearances), and in this different states have performed with different degrees of alacrity.

Sharp differences in institutional practices are also common in China. Huang (2008) has contrasted the private indigenous entrepreneurial model of Zhejiang province with the state-led capitalism of neighboring Shanghai or even Jiangsu province (with a prominent role for foreign investment). He considers the Shanghai model that has attracted a lot of attention the world over—as much as the skyscrapers of Pudong—as one of highly interventionist industrial policy, urban-biased, restricting the development of small-scale entrepreneurial businesses, privileging foreign, as opposed to indigenous, private business, and resulting in little innovation, rapid but relatively jobless growth, low labor income share, and high income inequality.

In this chapter we have focused on a few aspects of the nature of capitalism developing in the two countries. The major part of the economy in both countries is now in the private sector. But in terms of economic power, allocation of credit, and regulatory approvals, the state dominates the economy in China, though SOEs are now more commercialized than before; private business, though thriving, is often in a clientelistic relation with the state. In India the private corporate sector is more vigorous and autonomous than in China. In spite of some recognizable characteristics of the East Asian developmental state in both countries, they are actually quite different from that model in their own ways. As is expected in continent-size economies, the regional diversity on the capitalist path in both countries is also quite striking.

Chapter 7

Poverty and Inequality: How Is the Growth Shared?

In both China and India there is a general sense that much of the benefit of economic growth has been concentrated, that large masses of people are still very poor, and that the process of global integration of these two countries, for all the hype in the financial press, has left many people behind. In this chapter we discuss this issue with the help of the available empirical data and come to conclusions that are somewhat more ambiguous than are suggested in the popular discussion.

First, take the case of absolute poverty, the scourge of both countries for at least the past two centuries. There is a large literature on the intricacies[1] of poverty measurement: how to define a poverty line, if at all possible, and how it is related to local nutritional norms or the consumption basket of the poor; a head count of people below such a line does not capture the intensity of poverty among the different poor groups; there are large and increasing gaps between estimates of consumption expenditure derived from alternative sources such as national income accounts and household survey data (both of which have problems and are not quite comparable); what is an appropriate price index to use to deflate the monetary expenditure of the poor, and so on. For this chapter we shall largely ignore all this and draw on some crude head count poverty estimates on the basis of household survey data that are easily available.[2]

---

[1] See, for example, Srinivasan and Bardhan (1974), Lipton and Ravallion (1995), and Deaton and Kozel (2005).

[2] Note that for both countries the last year for which the survey data are available is

TABLE 6
Poverty Measures for $1 a Day Per Capita (In 2005 PPP)

Country	1981	1984	1987	1990	1993	1996	1999	2002	2005
Percentage of Population									
China	73.5	52.0	38.0	44.0	37.7	23.7	24.1	19.1	8.1
India	42.1	37.6	35.7	33.3	31.1	28.6	27.0	26.3	24.3
Number of People (in Millions)									
China	730.4	548.5	412.4	499.1	444.4	288.7	302.4	244.7	106.1
India	296.1	282.2	285.3	282.5	280.1	271.3	270.1	276.1	266.5

Source: Chen and Ravallion (2008)

Take, for example, the admittedly crude[3] poverty line of $1 a day[4] per capita (at 2005 purchasing power parity). With this poverty line, according to World Bank estimates, the proportion of people below it in China fell from 73.5 percent in 1981 to as low as 8.1 percent in 2005 (see table 6).

Those who do not want to use the World Bank estimates will get a qualitatively similar decline in poverty from Chinese official data, as in table 7.

Either way, this is a dramatic decline in a relatively short period. A part of this decline may not be real, as there may be some over-estimate of poverty in 1981 since there are grounds to believe that the official price deflator used for this estimation may not have been adequate for rural areas before 1985. But even a somewhat smaller decline still means nearly a half billion people lifted above the

2005, which means that they do not include the possible rise in poverty in the more recent years of sharply rising prices of food, fuel, and metals or the economic downturn.

[3] A poverty line like $1 per capita per day is an arbitrary cutoff with very little link to any estimate of the basic needs of the poor. Also, PPP calculations are not sensitive to the differential subsistence needs of the poor in different countries and cultural contexts. We still use this here because we do not have access to any alternative time series of poverty data that would allow us to compare across the two countries. We should, however, note that the qualitative results about the decline over time stated in the text will not change even if one uses the national estimates using local poverty lines in China and India, as we show later.

[4] The World Bank now recommends the use of a $1.25 per capita per day (at 2005 prices) poverty line. The $1 line, however, is closer to the official Indian poverty line. At the $1.25 poverty line, the percentage of people below it in 2005 was 42 percent in India and 16 percent in China.

TABLE 7

Percentage of People Below a Poverty Line, from Chinese Official Data

1981	1984	1987	1990	1993	1996	1999	2002	2005
52.8	24.1	16.8	22.2	20.0	9.8	7.6	7.3	5.2

Source: Ravallion and Chen (2007).
Note: Poverty line is defined here as 850 yuan per person per year in rural areas and 1,200 yuan in urban areas.

TABLE 8

Percentage of People Below a Poverty Line, from Indian Official Data

1983	1987–1988	1993–1994	2004–2005
45.2	39.3	35.8	27.5

Source: National Sample Survey.
Note: The official poverty line is supposed to be defined as supporting the consumption of 2,400 calories per person per day in rural areas and 2,100 calories in urban areas.

poverty line in less than a quarter century—an unparalleled achievement in world history.

As shown in table 6, the decline in the percentage of people below the $1 poverty line (in 2005 purchasing power parity) in India was from 42.1 percent in 1981 to 24.3 percent in 2005, a significant decline but not a dramatic one. Table 8 gives the corresponding percentages for selected years with the Indian official poverty line.

II

It is often claimed, both in the media and academia, that it was global integration that brought down the extreme poverty that had afflicted the two countries over many decades. While expansion of exports of labor-intensive manufactures probably lifted many people out of poverty in China in the past decade (not in India, where exports are still mainly skill- and capital-intensive), the more important reason for the dramatic decline of poverty over the past three decades may actually lie elsewhere. Table 6 suggests that more than half of the total decline in the numbers of poor people (below the poverty line of $1 a day per capita) in China between 1981 and 2005 had already happened by the mid-1980s, *before* the big strides in foreign trade and investment in China in the 1990s and later. Much of the extreme poverty was concentrated in rural areas, and its large decline in the first half of the 1980s is perhaps mainly a result of the spurt in agricultural growth following decollectivization and one of history's most egalitarian land redistributions, with every rural family getting an equal piece of land (subject to differences in family size and regional average), in addition to an upward readjustment of farm procurement prices—these are mostly internal factors that had very little to do with global integration.[5] To settle the issue of how much of the poverty decline is due to globalization and how much due to largely domestic factors, one needs causal models, which have not been econometrically tested much in the literature. In an attempt to econometrically measure, on the basis of a time series of province-level data, the effects of different factors on rural poverty reduction in China, Fan, Zhang, and Zhang (2004) show that since the mid-1980s domestic public investment (particularly in education, agricultural research and development, roads, and other rural infrastructure) has been the dominant factor both in growth and in rural poverty reduction, much more than economic reform. With a new provincial panel dataset Montalvo and Ravallion (forthcoming)

[5] In the 1980s there was some trade expansion; for example, the export to GDP ratio went up from about 7 percent in 1981 to 12 percent in 1989. But labor-intensive manufactures were still not very important in Chinese exports; in the first half of the 1980s minerals and other natural resource–intensive products formed a substantial fraction of exports. In 1985, for example, the largest single export was petroleum. The mean tariff rate declined only slightly in the 1980s, from 31.9 percent in 1980–1983 to 29.2 percent in 1988–1990. The big decline in tariff rates started only around 1992; the range of commodities regulated by quotas and import licenses actually expanded over the 1980s. In any case, the proportion of the labor force in manufacturing in this period was small, so the large poverty decline in the first half of the 1980s is unlikely to be attributable to manufacturing exports. It is also worth noting that, after the sharp drop between 1981 and 1987, the poverty percentage went up or remained the same between 1987 and 1993. This indicates that by 1987 the agricultural spurt had worked itself out and the effect of labor-intensive manufactures was still weak. It was only after 1993 that the poverty percentage again started to decline; labor-intensive exports may have played a significant role in this decline, although even in this period one should not minimize the effect of largely domestic factors such as easier migration from rural areas and higher agricultural procurement prices.

confirm econometrically that the poverty reduction in China has been mainly due to agricultural growth.

In India, NSS data suggest that the rate of decline in poverty did not accelerate in 1993–2005, the period of intensive opening of the economy, compared to the 1970s and 1980s. This may be connected with the fact that agricultural output (and TFP) grew at a slower rate in the past decade compared to the earlier decade (see table 2 in chapter 2). This may be largely on account of the decline in public investment in rural infrastructure (such as irrigation, roads, and prevention of soil erosion), which has little to do with globalization. NSS data also suggest that there has been a decline in the rate of growth of real wages in the period 1993–2005 compared to the previous decade, 1983–1993. We should also recognize that private consumer expenditure data of the NSS that are used in poverty estimates (as with the Chinese household survey data) do not capture the declining access to environmental resources (such as forests, fisheries, grazing lands, and water both for drinking and irrigation) on which the daily lives and livelihoods of the poor depend.

Global integration does not seem to have helped some of the other nonincome indicators such as those of health. The National Family Health Survey (NFHS) data show that some of India's health indicators are worse than those of Bangladesh (in maternal mortality, infant mortality, child immunization rates, etc.), and even those of sub-Saharan Africa (in the percentage of underweight children), in spite of much higher growth rates in India than in those other countries. The percentage of underweight children (younger than age three) is 46 in India, and about 30 percent on average in sub-Saharan Africa (8 percent in China). Take the case of Gujarat, one of the richest, highest-growth, and highest-reform states in India: the percentage of underweight children, which was already high (higher than sub-Saharan Africa), went *up* between NFHS 2 (1998–1999) and NFHS 3 (2005–2006).[6]

---

[6] There is some discrepancy between the NFHS data and those reported by the National Nutrition Monitoring Bureau (NNMB), not in the levels of malnutrition in 2005–2006, but in the trends over time. One should note that the NNMB surveys have a smaller sample size and are limited to ten states.

Some disaggregated studies[7] across districts in India have also found trade liberalization actually slowing down the decline in rural poverty. Such results may indicate the difficulty of displaced farmers and workers in adjusting to new activities and sectors on account of various constraints (for example, in getting credit or information or infrastructural facilities such as power and roads, high incidence of school dropouts, and labor market rigidities), even when new opportunities are opened up by globalization. This is in line with textbooks in international economics that emphasize that product-market liberalization need not be an improvement when there are severe distortions in input markets (such as those of credit, labor, electricity, land, etc. in the case of India).

India's pace of poverty reduction has been less than China's, not just because growth has been faster in China but also because the same 1 percent growth rate reduces (or is associated with reduction in) poverty in India by much less. This so-called growth elasticity of poverty reduction is much higher in China than in India; this may have something to do[8] with the differential inequalities of opportunity in the two countries. We do not have good measures of inequality of opportunity,[9] but in a poor agrarian economy such inequality is largely reflected in that of land and education. Contrary to common perception, these inequalities are much higher in India than in China.

As noted in chapter 3, the Gini coefficient of inequality of land distribution (in terms of operational holdings) in rural India was 0.62 in 2002; the corresponding figure in China was 0.49 in 2002. India's educational inequality is among the worst in the world: according to a table in the *World Development Report 2006*, published by the World Bank, the Gini coefficient of the distribution of adult schooling years in the population, a crude measure of educational inequality, was 0.56 in India in 1998–2000, which is not just higher

---

[7] For example, Topalova (2007). In an unpublished comment, T. N. Srinivasan has raised some doubts about the methods in this study.

[8] Other important factors that may be operative here include those that restrict labor-intensive industrialization in India, such as those discussed in chapter 2.

[9] Most of the income or consumption inequality estimates that are usually cited are those of inequality of outcome, not of opportunity.

than 0.37 in China in 2000, but even higher than almost all Latin American countries (for example, Brazil: 0.39), and some African countries. Because of the educational disparity among households, a study of the determinants of rural poverty in China and India by Borooah, Gustafsson, and Shi (2006) finds that education has a much bigger impact on poverty in India than in China. Apart from land and education, the other important ingredient of inequality of opportunity is due to ethnicity. In China, ethnic minorities make up only about 9 percent of the population. In India, with a much more heterogeneous society, about one-third of the population is in socially disadvantaged minority categories (such as Muslims, "dalits," and tribal people), and thus minority status is a more important determinant of poverty in India than in China.

Comparing across states in India, as Datt and Ravallion (2002) point out, the growth elasticity of poverty reduction depends on the initial distribution of land and human capital. Purfield (2006) indicates that in the period 1977–2001 this elasticity was quite low in high-growth states such as Maharashtra and Karnataka, and high in states such as Kerala and West Bengal. Comparing across states and over time, Topalova (2008) estimates that "inclusiveness" of growth (measured by her as the difference between the growth in consumption of the bottom 30 percent of the population and the top 30 percent) depends significantly and positively on the share of the population that has completed primary and particularly secondary education, apart from financial development, flexible labor markets, and infrastructure in the state. Similarly, comparing across provinces in China, Ravallion and Chen (2007) find that growth had more poverty-reducing impact in provinces that initially had less inequality.

III

What about the link between market reform and inequality? At least two major problems beset the analyst in this matter. One is that so many other changes have taken place in the past quarter century of reform, it is difficult to disentangle the effects of reform from those of other ongoing changes (such as technological progress—often information-based or skill-biased—which usually changes the income distribution in favor of the better-off skilled labor groups, demographic changes, or macroeconomic policies). The second is that in both countries there are reasons to suspect that economic inequality (or its rise) could be underestimated (though not necessarily) in view of a widely noted fact facing household surveys (in many countries) of large (and increasing) nonresponse by the rich households. In addition there is reason to believe that the income data may not have adequately covered the rising importance of family-run businesses in China, which results in understating the rise in inequality. It is also difficult to compare inequality in China[10] and India, as most of the inequality data that are cited in this context usually are for income inequality in China and consumption expenditure inequality in India (as the Indian NSS does not collect income data).[11] Consumption expenditure data do show a rise in expenditure inequality in both countries in the past decade or so. But, as we have suggested, this rise may be an underestimate, and there is very little analysis as yet to show that this rise is primarily due to economic reform.

Even if economic reform were to be causally linked with higher growth, the link between growth and inequality is not always clear. In China, as Chaudhuri and Ravallion (2006) show, the periods of rapid growth did not necessarily bring more rapid increases in income inequality; the periods of falling inequality (1981–1985 and 1995–1998) had among the highest growth rates in average household income. In both countries, periods of high agricultural growth may have reduced overall inequality, since the agricultural sector usually has lower inequality than the nonagricultural sector. The

---

[10] According to an estimate by Lin et al. (2008), that, unlike most other estimates, takes into account cost of living differences between rural and urban areas and across provinces, the national Gini coefficient of income inequality in China increased from 0.29 in 1990 to 0.39 in 2004, as mentioned in chapter 1.

[11] The National Council of Applied Economic Research data, which occasionally provide income data, suggest that (after correction for rural-urban price variation) the Gini coefficient for inequality of Indian income was 0.535 in 2004–2005, much higher than that in China.

recent decline in agricultural growth rates may have had some influence in the rising inequality in both countries, which may not have much direct connection with market reform as such.

For the urban sector in India, figure 9 plots changes, over the period 1983–2004, in the real wage rate for urban full-time employees by level of education, and shows a faster rate of increase in the wage rate for those with higher education. According to the estimates by the Asian Development Bank (2007), the Gini coefficient of average real wages of urban full-time employees in India increased from 0.38 in 1983 to 0.47 in 2004. This increase in wage inequality is consistent with the skill-intensity of Indian economic growth (in which reforms may have played some role) and the looming talent shortage that the corporate sector complains about.

In urban China also the rate of return to college (and graduate) education compared to, say, high school education has more than doubled since the early 1990s. On the basis of household survey data in six provinces, Zhang et al. (2005) report that college graduates earned 12.2 percent more than senior high school graduates in 1988, but 37.3 percent more in 2001. In both China and India, here again it is difficult to separate the effect of skill-biased technological progress from that of economic reform.

Beyond the discussion of wage inequality, while real wage rates have increased in both countries (much more in China than in India), it is quite likely that with market reform general workers may have experienced much more "churning" in the industrial labor market, particularly in China; but protests by organized workers against layoffs are more subdued in China. Strikes are not permitted, and the monopoly Party union has hardly any say in layoffs by employers. China laid off about thirty million workers from state- and collective-owned urban manufacturing enterprises in just five years, 1995–2000; this is unparalleled in the world history of the industrial working class, and unthinkable in India.

The official unemployment estimates are not comparable between the two countries. According to a somewhat more comparable estimate on the basis of household survey data by Giles, Park, and Zhang (2005), the unemployment rate of urban permanent

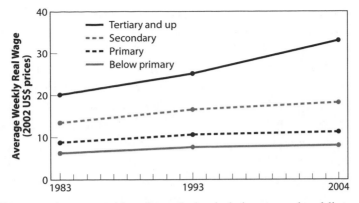

Figure 9. Average weekly real wage by level of education, urban full-time employees, India (2002 U.S.$ prices). Source: Asian Development Bank (2007)

residents in China was 11.1 percent in 2002. In India, according to NSS data, the urban unemployment rate was about 6 percent in 2004–2005. (In both estimates the reference period is the last week.) The much higher unemployment rate in urban China may be due to those massive layoffs from public enterprises in the second half of the 1990s. From a sample survey in thirteen cities, Appleton et al. (2002) find that of all the retrenched workers since 1992, 53 percent still remained unemployed in early 2000. Since then, however, the urban unemployment rate apparently has declined significantly, at least until the recent economic downturn, when by all accounts unemployment has risen steeply, particularly in globally exposed coastal China.

Since reform arguably has been more "urban-biased" in India and (at least since the 1990s) in China, one may look at the urban-rural disparity. The ratio of urban to rural mean income (or consumption) is higher in China than India, and it is rising in India, but the increase in disparity in China is attenuated when one takes into account the rural-urban differences in cost of living.[12] Lin et al.

[12] Sicular et al. (2007) estimate the urban-rural income ratio to be 2.1, after adjusting for spatial price differences. Another statistical problem is that the rural-urban definitions of households in China are somewhat uncertain because (a) rural areas are increasingly being reclassified as urban in official data, and (b) the location of households by residence is different from that by registration (in view of the restrictions of the *hukou* system).

(2008) decompose national inequality in China (measured by the Theil index), after taking into account cost of living differences, into inequality within each of the rural and urban sectors and inequality between the rural and urban sectors. It seems that both intraurban and urban-rural disparities contribute to recent increases in income inequality. The contribution of intraurban inequality to total inequality rose from 15.7 percent in 1990 to 34 percent in 2004; that of intrarural inequality fell from 72.2 percent to 35.6 percent; and that of urban-rural inequality rose from 12.1 percent to 30.4 percent. It should be noted that the urban population in China also gained disproportionately from the privatization (at highly subsidized prices) and marketization of housing since the mid-1990s.

As we discuss in the next chapter, in China the urban-rural disparity in social services increased in the postreform period, with a near-collapse of the rural social services, whereas in urban areas social services, though weaker than before, still serve the majority of the resident (and working) urban population. The decline of rural health services in China (along with the one-child policy[13]) may also have had some effect on gender equity in life chances. Male to female ratio in children (younger than six years) is very high at about 1.19 in China[14] (1.08 in India). But one should add that female literacy and labor participation rates (above 70 percent in urban China, 24 percent in urban India) being substantially higher in China, women in China have had the opportunity to contribute to economic growth much more than in India.

Regional disparity in income (or consumption) is greater in China than in India. But over the past two decades, China's backward regions have grown at rates almost comparable to its advanced regions, and regional earning disparities may be narrowing (though not yet per capita income disparities). Initiatives such as the Western Development Program supported large infrastructure building

---

[13] This policy may also have resulted in some underreporting of girls, apart from inducing gender-specific abortions.

[14] Unlike in India, where the gender imbalance in the population is greater in some of the better-off regions in the northwest, in China it is greater in some of the worse-off regions (such as the southeast).

in remote regions; and the mobility-restricting effects of the *hukou* system may be weakening. In any case, Benjamin et al. (2008) have shown on the basis of analyzing the survey data collected by the Research Center for Rural Economy that the contribution of inter-provincial inequality in total inequality in China is smaller than is usually thought. Decomposing total national income inequality into between-province and within-province components after adjusting for cost of living differences, Lin et al. (2008) estimate that the for-mer contributed only 11 percent.

In India the poorer states (largely concentrated in the central and eastern regions) have grown much more slowly than richer states (mostly in the west and the south), so relative inequality has increased.[15] In general, reform has advanced more smoothly in the west and the south of India, and better reform implementation in a state may have gone hand-in-hand with better initial infrastructure. Of course, with the removal of industrial licensing, which ostensibly used to give some weight to regional backwardness, private capital will move more to states where policies are business-friendly and infrastructure is better.

In China provinces with more global exposure and higher growth did not have the larger increase in inequality. As Benjamin et al. (2008) show, while the Gini coefficient of income in coastal China increased from 0.35 in 1991 to 0.39 in 2000, it increased from 0.39 to 0.48 in the interior provinces.[16] In the coastal provinces, more rapid job growth in the nonstate sector helped reduce the urban-rural income differential there.

But within-village inequality often rises in areas (particularly in backward areas) where poorer households are less able to participate in the booming nonfarm growth (possibly on account of deficiencies in skill and access to credit and marketing networks). For example the TVEs have been concentrated more in the eastern and coastal

[15] Decomposition of inequality of per capita consumption across states suggests, however, that the between-states inequality is still a very small proportion of the total inequality.

[16] The estimates by Lin et al. (2008) show that the results are somewhat modified in the comparison of the coastal and western regions if one adjusts for cost of living differences and extends the period to 2004.

regions.[17] Although India has had much less rural industrialization, in general rural industries have thrived more in regions that were already better off.

Finally, let us comment on one aspect of dynamic inequality on which there is very little comparative evidence or analysis, and yet in the long run it may be more important than the static inequality data that are usually cited. This relates to intergenerational mobility, which is likely to be much higher in China than in India. Khor and Pencavel (2006) found (subject to many qualifications they themselves cite for their estimates) that the degree of income mobility in urban China in the first half of the 1990s was much higher than that in the United States, and it increased between 1990 and 1995.[18] Contrast that with the usual statements about static inequality, which usually point the other way. Ding and Wang (2008) in a decomposition of the measurement of absolute income mobility in China for the period 1989–2000 show that a considerable part of the mobility is due to high growth. We don't know of any comparable study of mobility in India. One sociological study of occupational mobility by Kumar, Heath, and Heath (2002) on the basis of socioeconomic data (for urban and rural males) collected over the period 1971–1996 in connection with the National Election Survey finds that while there has been some change in the occupational distribution (associated with the decline of agriculture) and some new opportunities for social advancement have opened up, there has been no systematic additional weakening of the links between the class positions of fathers and their sons. In terms of caste mobility over two generations, they find some modest evidence of an improvement in the chances of dalits (one of the lowest caste groups, confined earlier mostly to menial jobs) of getting into the salaried class, but not for other socially disadvantaged groups.

In this chapter, after describing the decline in poverty (dramatic in China, solid in India), we showed that the relationship between

[17] In the inequality among rural households reported in Khan (2004), more than half was attributable to inequality in rural nonagricultural income (both wage and business income). Rural industrialization also drains skilled labor from backward villages, and their remittances go primarily to better-off households in those villages.

[18] Of course, looking only at income mobility in urban China cannot capture whatever influence the mobility restrictions of the *hukou* system still had.

poverty reduction and market reform or globalization is more ambiguous than is usually claimed. The impact of growth on poverty reduction is weaker in India than in China, probably on account of initial conditions, including larger inequality (of opportunity) in India, owing to inequalities of land, education, and social status. The link between economic reform and inequality is also ambiguous and difficult to disentangle from the effects of other ongoing changes. There is some limited evidence of significant intergenerational mobility in China, but not much in India.

Chapter 8

The Social Sector:
The Relevance of the Socialist Legacy

In some basic indicators of the social sector China is clearly more advanced than India, but this is one area where the Chinese differential advance was achieved in the socialist period and, if anything, the period of market reform has eroded some of this advance. We shall focus on two parts of this sector, health and education. Even those who are primarily interested in economic growth will agree that these two basic ingredients of human capital in a population are crucial not just for current well-being but for long-term development and worker productivity as well. In both of these spheres there are some egregious failures of both market and government in most countries, but they have been particularly acute in China and India. We shall discuss the problems in the larger context of the political and economic structure in the two countries and show that the structural deficiencies from which they arise are similar as well as different in the two cases.

In most broad aggregative measures of health outcomes China's performance has been much better than India's, and it has been so for several decades. For example, life expectancy at birth now in India is what it used to be in China in the early 1970s, before the onset of reform. In infant mortality, by 1975 China had achieved a rate that India had not reached even in 2000. To this we may add, to repeat from chapter 7, that of India's children under the age of three, as many as 46 percent are underweight,[1] compared to China's 8 percent. The mortality rate of children under the age of five in India is more than twice that in China. Maternal mortality rate (per hundred thousand live births) in India has been almost ten times that in China.[2] In India, malnutrition among women (particularly evident in the very large incidence of anemia, already among the worst in the world) increased between 1998–1999 and 2005–2006, according to the data from National Family Health Survey, in a period of high economic growth. This increase is quite substantial even in high-growth states such as Gujarat. More than 1.5 million Indian children die every year due to waterborne diseases such as diarrhea and dysentery.

There are, of course, some differences in initial conditions between the two countries. India being in general nearer the tropics than most of China is, one would expect a larger incidence of certain diseases in India, and conditions of vector control may be more difficult, other things being equal. According to World Health Organization estimates for 1998, the burden of infectious and parasitic diseases (measured in terms of disability-adjusted life years per capita) is seven times as high in India as in China. This may be partly the result of differences in physical and climatic conditions, but only partly, as it is also partly an outcome of relative policy deficiency. Socialist China had a much more vigorous policy for public health and sanitation than India, and also a larger army of paramedics pressed into basic public-health service in the villages (which took care of easily treated diseases and injuries, with some regions having a system of referrals to higher-level medical services for more difficult cases). By the mid-1970s China had a rudimentary system of medical insurance (called "cooperative medical scheme") that covered the overwhelming majority of rural people, something that did not exist in India. Also, the Chinese government showed an

[1] In weight-for-age measures, "underweight" refers to weights at least two standard deviations below the median.

[2] The percentage of births attended by skilled health personnel in China has been twice that in India.

ability to mobilize campaigns for preventive health care and against public-health threats that were impressive by the standards of most developing countries.

In contrast, India after Independence has never had a system of public health and sanitation anywhere on that scale. There has been no systematic planning and delivery of public-health services (as opposed to curative medical services) or sustained large-scale disease control. As Dasgupta (2005) points out, in India "there is strong capacity for dealing with (disease) outbreaks when they occur, but not to prevent them from occurring. Impressive capacity also exists for conducting intensive campaigns, but not for sustaining these gains on a continuing basis after the campaign. This is illustrated by the near-eradication of malaria through highly-organized efforts in the 1950s, and its resurgence when attention shifted to other priorities such as family planning."

This public-health and preventive care situation is not entirely unconnected to the very different political-economy factors in India and in China in the early socialist decades. With the advance of antibiotics, the elite in India felt less threatened than in the past by the spread of communicable diseases among the poor, leading to a policy deemphasis on environmental hygiene, and the elite succeeded in diverting public funds to high-end curative treatment in big urban hospitals, away from rudimentary but effective and widespread health services in the villages of the kind China used to have.

But in the past quarter century of economic reform there has been a sea change in public-health policy in China. With decollectivization in 1978–1979 the rural health services collapsed. The paramedics who used to be paid in work points at the production brigade and team levels now lacked a systematic method of compensation. Soon the total number of paramedics fell to less than a quarter of what it had been in the 1970s. By the mid-1980s the "cooperative medical scheme" covered less than 10 percent of the rural population (most of it in the better-off coastal areas). In general, with the collapse of local public finances, particularly in remote rural areas, fewer resources were devoted to public health. There was a decline even in curative services; the total number of hospital beds per thousand rural residents in 2003 was about half of what it had been twenty years earlier. Yet those twenty years saw phenomenal economic growth in China. While the basic indicators of public health kept on improving (with rising income, nutrition, education and transportation), the pace of improvement was slower than before, and was particularly bad for rural girls. For example, between 1981 and 2000, while the infant mortality rate for boys decreased from 40 per thousand to 25.8, that for girls decreased much less, from 38.1 to 36.7. Preventive care declined as government funds for disease control and prevention decreased from 0.11 percent of GDP in 1978 to 0.04 percent by 1993 (and it has decreased further in subsequent years). The incidence of some contagious diseases—such as hepatitis, schistosomiasis, and pulmonary TB, in addition to HIV—has increased.

In this period China essentially moved from one of the most impressive basic public-health coverage systems in the world to in effect a privatized (or user charge–financed) system,[3] particularly in rural areas. In the cities, formal-sector employees have some form of health insurance, but there too premiums and fees paid by patients have increased considerably over time. Private health insurance has started, but in 2003 it covered less than 6 percent of the population. Obviously, the poor have had to bear the brunt of all this, as even in the cities most of them are in the uncovered part of the population, migrants and informal-sector workers. Yip and Mahal (2008) point out that 76 percent of the lowest-income quintile of urban individuals do not have health insurance; the corresponding percentage in the lowest-income quintile of rural individuals is 80 percent. This implies that many sick people do not seek medical care, largely on account of financial hardship. Yip and Mahal cite data that in 2003 nearly half of those reporting an illness did not seek outpatient care. Those who did spent an inordinate proportion of their income on health care; according to their data, the poorest-quintile individuals in rural areas spend as much as 27 percent of their income on health care, and in the poorest urban quintile it is 11 percent.

---

[3] This was the case even before the recent appearance of openly for-profit hospitals and clinics. It is reported that 72 percent of clinics in China are now for-profit.

This large change in the public funding basis of health services in China is linked with a systemic problem relating to decentralized development. As discussed in chapter 2, China is a glowing example of industrialization under decentralization. But one side effect of economic decentralization is acute regional inequality. Coastal China surged ahead, and local governments there flush with profits from the TVEs under their control could buttress social services as their funding from communes disintegrated all over the country. But the interior or agriculture-dominant provinces and remote areas, where TVEs were few and profitable ones even fewer, were largely left to their own devices in funding social services. There was a highly inadequate block grant from upper levels of government, and medical facilities were encouraged to generate as much revenue as they could (often from drug sales, test fees, and unnecessary procedures),[4] the surplus from which they were allowed to keep or pay the staff in the form of bonuses. Informal payments from patients (sometimes called "red packages")[5] and kickbacks from drug wholesalers have been rampant.

Then the fiscal reforms of 1994 centralized revenue collection and allocation, and many local areas were left with unfunded mandates for basic social services including education and health care. The fiscal reforms of more recent years clamped down on some of the arbitrary fees and taxes that many local governments had imposed on the local population, leaving them more financially strapped. Increasing regional disparity in provision of health care is indicated by the fact that in 1985 the total number of technical medical personnel per thousand people was somewhat lower in cities than in the surrounding counties; twenty years later, it was more than twice in cities than in counties. It is also no coincidence that, as Yip and Mahal (2008) estimate, the crude measures of interprovincial inequality (such as the coefficient of variation) in aggregative health

---

[4] For example, the percentage rate of births by cesarean section (a more expensive procedure) has multiplied several times since the onset of market reforms.

[5] It is reported that more than 70 percent of hospital patients in China have to make these informal payments; the reported figures in India are much smaller, though not insignificant.

outcomes such as life expectancy at birth or infant mortality increased in the twenty years following 1980.

While China moved away from its egalitarian and impressive basic health-care service of the socialist period, India's health-care service remained dismal and inegalitarian throughout. Only about 15 percent of the people in India have any health insurance (primarily through their employers), and the share of out-of-pocket spending in total spending on health care exceeds 70 percent, which is higher[6] than in China (though it has increased faster in the latter country). Appearances to the contrary, health care in India is predominantly private and largely unregulated. Household survey data suggest that 85 percent of all visits for health care in rural areas, even by the poorest people, are to private practitioners; about 60 percent of all hospitalizations in India are in private hospitals. While the poor quality of service in public clinics and hospitals (and absenteeism by nurses and doctors) often drive patients to private doctors[7] (some of them quacks or crooks) in India, in China the high fees charged in public-health clinics (and their concentration on revenue-generating activities) in effect turn them into for-profit private providers. In India, unlike China, at least the public facilities receive the bulk of their revenue from government subsidies and they provide their (often paltry and poor-quality) services at low cost to those who are too poor to afford more expensive private care (although rampant corruption renders the public service provided not entirely free). China, however, unlike India, has had a long tradition of training and licensing village doctors. The Indian system is more top-down: Although health-care delivery is largely in the jurisdiction of the state governments, most of their budget is spent on staff salaries and they are thus much more dependent on the central government both for general health-care plans and priorities and for nonsalary items of public-health expenditure. Also, as a part

[6] More than 90 percent of per capita spending on health care is private, not just in socially backward states such as Uttar Pradesh but also in states such as Kerala, which has good public-health facilities.

[7] There has been very little attempt to train them or help them qualify for minimum licensing arrangements. Professional medical associations have not generally been helpful in this respect.

of reorientation of those priorities, the fraction of total health-care spending on control of communicable diseases has declined over the years, leading to a reemergence of some of those diseases.

In both countries doctors often overmedicate and refer patients for unnecessary diagnostic tests and procedures, driving up health-care costs in general. This is part of a general market failure in health care, in which the decider (the doctor) is not the purchaser (the patient), and may have a financial interest in dispensing medicines or performing tests. In poor countries with little information and education, the problem is exacerbated as the patients themselves sometimes show a preference for unnecessary antibiotics and ste-roids, which the quacks oblige. In both countries the more impor-tant problem is a governance failure. The public-health delivery system is afflicted with poor provider incentives coupled with little accountability to patients.[8]

First, medical personnel are often paid a fixed salary indepen-dent of the number of patients or the number of patient visits, so they have no economic incentive to serve patients. In India, doctors in public hospitals are allowed to practice in private as well, which biases their financial incentives toward focusing their efforts on serv-ing their private patients.[9] In China, some of doctors' nonfixed salary comes from commissions on drug sales, with effects on overprescrip-tion. Second, there is little monitoring or punishment for laxity in service in either country. Third, the poor have very little organized "voice" in sanctioning errant providers in either country. In the oth-erwise vibrant democracy of India, in most areas local democracy is not strong enough to keep public service providers accountable to the local citizens. Periodic elections provide a rather blunt instru-ment for keeping public officials in check, and in any case the elec-toral agenda is full of different pressing issues, of which poor health service is only one. Besides, politicians find it easier to claim credit for inaugurating a big hospital or installing new equipment there

---

[8] For an elaboration of these issues in the context of India, see Hammer, Aiyar, and Samji (2007).

[9] In China, public hospital doctors are allowed to do contract work for other hospitals on their days off.

than for regular maintenance of services or public sanitation and vector control. In China, the channels of local accountability are even weaker. In both countries, local social groups and nongovernmental organizations (NGOs) provide some accountability pressure in localized pockets (more in India than in China).

II

In education, the contours of the basic story in both countries are similar to those in health care in many respects. Socialist China had an active policy of spreading literacy and basic skills among the general population,[10] to an extent unmatched by India. In 1982, even after the chaotic years of the Cultural Revolution, two-thirds of the adult population in China was literate or semiliterate, at a time when in India more than half the population was illiterate. The average years of schooling in the Indian population older than age fifteen in 2000 was less than what China had already achieved by the beginning of the 1980s. Of course, relative spending in India used to favor higher education somewhat (just as health-care spending favored urban hospitals and curative medicine). In 1982, less than 1 percent of adults in China had any college education at all, while India had three times as many college graduates per capita as China. The Cultural Revolution, which can be described as, among other things, an episode of one of the largest destructions of human capital in history, wreaked havoc particularly on higher education. (In the area of health, the catastrophic disruption was the Great Famine in the early 1960s). In the reform period China has tried to make amends by dramatically expanding attainment particularly in higher education. By 2004, 6.7 percent of adults had some tertiary education. Of general secondary school graduates, only 4.6 percent enrolled in a regular institution of higher education in 1980; by 2000 that had increased

---

[10] Of course, education did not significantly increase income; Communist Party membership mattered more for improving income. In the past two decades the rate of return to education has increased, but there is evidence that returns to Communist Party membership did not diminish.

to 73.2 percent. India also accelerated enrollment in higher education, but not as rapidly. As in the health area, decentralized financing
of education in China made things difficult for local governments,
particularly in rural and remote areas, to keep up with the mandated
educational expansion, and the requisite increased school fees made
things difficult for the poor for many years. Thus educational disparities increased in the reform period, and differential schooling has
now become a major source of widening class division in China.

More than half of adult women are illiterate in India; in China,
only around 10 percent are illiterate. For all its brilliant scientists
and software engineers, India is the largest single-country contributor to the pool of illiterate people (and school dropouts) in the
world. Only about half of India's children have completed eight
years of education by age fifteen.[11] One-fifth of India's children in
the five to fourteen age group are not in school. Youth illiteracy has
been a special problem in India for many years (it is greater even
than that in many African countries). In the twenty-five to twenty-
nine age group, for example, China has only negligible illiteracy left,
whereas in India about 30 percent are still illiterate. Household survey data in India suggest that the secondary school attendance rate
at ages sixteen and seventeen is 50 percent higher for the richest expenditure group compared to the poorest, and three-quarters of the
difference results from higher attendance in private schools by the
richer children. Lower attendance of poorer children is partly due to
supply-side problems (distance to school, teacher absenteeism, lack
of remedial programs for poorly performing students and especially
for girls, lack of safety in the journey to and from school, and lack
of toilets in schools), in addition to the usual demand-side problems
(poverty that makes teenagers drop out in order to earn something
for the family or, in the case of girls, to take care of household chores
when the mother is working, and social discrimination that works
against girls' education). In fact, India's educational inequality is
among the worst in the world, as mentioned in chapter 7.

---

[11] As for quality of education, one dismal indicator noted by Pratham, a large education
NGO, is that even in fifth grade some 35 percent of the children cannot read or write.

In China, private schools have grown rapidly in recent years, particularly for secondary education in urban areas. The share of total education funds for all levels coming from government budgets dropped from 84 percent in 1991 to 62 percent in 2004. Among the nonbudgeted items, tuition fees alone grew from 4 percent of educational expenditures in 1991 to about 19 percent by 2004. Inability to pay school fees became a major source of educational disadvantage for the poor. Girls are still at a disadvantage in number of years of school, although gender disparity in education seems to be decreasing.

We have already referred to the increased emphasis on higher education in both countries. But less than 10 percent of the eighteen to twenty-three age group enroll in higher education institutions in India (compared to more than 20 percent in China). Of course, even a microscopic minority that is highly educated in a large country is sizable in absolute number and can make a splash in the world markets—for example, it has been reported for some time that there are more IT workers in Bangalore now than in Silicon Valley in California. But the sustainability of this for India as a whole is in some doubt, particularly when the majority of higher education institutions in the country are currently dysfunctional. The student's university performance as signal of quality is increasingly replaced by that in competitive examinations outside. The higher education institutions are strapped for government funds,[12] and yet ways of mobilizing private resources for public institutions remain largely blocked. They are overregulated in most academic decisions and often hopelessly politicized, and low in research productivity (measured, for example, by top journal citation index) in science and technology. As figure 10 shows, in terms of the number of research articles published in top-quality international journals by resident researchers China has now outpaced India. In the 2008 Times Higher Education ranking of world universities in terms of academic reputation and performance, the list of the top one hundred universities included two from China and none from India.

[12] In contrast, state financing for higher education more than doubled in China in just five years, between 1998 and 2003.

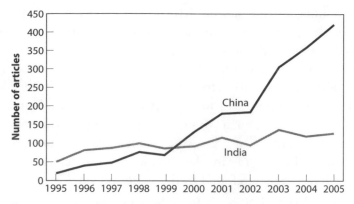

Figure 10. Articles published in high-impact journals by India- and China-based authors. Source: Organisation for Economic Co-operation and Development (2007)

Both in research and development expenditure as a percentage of GDP and number of patents taken out, China is far ahead of India. It is projected that by the early 2010s, China will surpass the United States and Japan in applications for new patents (particularly in the areas of chemical engineering, digital computers, and telephone and data transmission).

Already a talent shortage is reported to have hit India's capital goods industry, and even for the IT-related sector it is believed in some quarters that the reservoir of India's technical and managerial skills may prove rather shallow in the near future.[13] In any case, companies often have to put the engineering graduates they hire through long, intensive training programs to make them employable for their purposes.

In both countries there is now a renewed effort on the part of the government to press more resources into and improve the delivery of public education and health-care services. The Chinese

---

[13] According to the McKinsey Global Institute, talent shortages are looming in both China and India. China is producing more engineering graduates than India, but the proportion of them who are, according to the study, "suitable" for professional jobs, particularly at the international standard, is somewhat higher in India than in China. In 2003 the total number of "suitable" young engineers (excluding civil and agricultural engineers but including those with IT and computer science degrees) was 160 thousand in China and 130 thousand in India.

program seems more ambitious, in attempting to provide partially subsidized universal basic health care[14] and a program of free universal and compulsory education for nine years, and the Chinese government has more budgetary resources to devote to this. There is a new county-level voluntary health insurance scheme afoot, known as the New Cooperative Medical Scheme. In particular, its aim is to insure rural residents against catastrophic health-care expenses. The National Rural Health Mission in India plans to more than double the government spending on health care, with the purpose specifically of increasing access to primary health care for the rural poor. The major initiative to universalize education in India particularly at the primary and lower secondary levels is the recently launched Sarva Shiksha Abhiyan ("education for all" campaign).

But in both countries the governance and accountability issues mentioned earlier will not be resolved easily. In India, the weakness of local democracy (in terms of autonomy, funds, and administrative personnel), coupled with a corrupt and inert bureaucracy, dissipates many a well-intentioned policy measure from above. In China, it remains to be seen how effective and adequate the actual implementation of the ambitious program will be and how much the current burden of most of the revenues of public hospitals being extracted from patients will be reduced. Over the past several years, the constant chanting of the "harmonious society" mantra by the central leadership has not always succeeded in reining in local officials from their hitherto single-minded, frantic (and lucrative) pursuit of income growth often at the expense of social welfare. In any case, the latter are not too enthusiastic about the large share of the proposed increase in funding to be matched from local government coffers. Without a fundamental change in the way rural hospitals and schools are funded, poorer areas will still have a great deal of difficulty in scraping together local financing, even with a somewhat larger financial commitment by the central and provincial governments (which so far has mainly covered the loss of local

[14] Recently the government announced that this policy will be accelerated as part of the domestic demand stimulus program, since health-care uncertainties motivate a significant part of precautionary saving, particularly in rural China.

revenue from the abolition of agricultural taxes and miscellaneous fees).

In both countries, the basic problem of equity and quality of social services remains when both the bureaucracy and the provider are bound to act out of self-interest if their incentive systems are not restructured, and when the intended beneficiaries are not well informed about what is best for them and often lack the "voice" or power to sanction, even when they are.

Chapter 9

Environment: The Alarming Signs

The environment includes many different aspects of nature and the ecosystem that envelops human life, even though most public discussion currently tends to concentrate on issues around global warming. In this chapter we shall focus mainly on the local commons that affect the daily lives and livelihoods of many poor people in China and India. Local environmental resources include the quality of air and water as basic necessities of life as well as the conditions of the village commons such as forests, fisheries, agricultural land, and irrigation, which are particularly important for the rural poor. For comparative purposes we need some quantitative indexes for these different aspects of environment in the two countries. Table 9 provides some aggregate information regarding different indicators of environment, based on calculations by the Yale University Center for Environmental Law and Policy and the Columbia University Center for International Earth Science Information Network. These are, of course, necessarily crude measures, which through their methods of standardization and aggregation lose many important local particularities and nuances, but they give us a rough comparative picture.

The overall environment performance score for China in 2008 is 65.1 (with rank 105 out of 149 countries), somewhat better than that of India's 60.3 (with rank 120). For comparison, the highest score among these countries is for Switzerland, 95.5, and the lowest is for Niger, 39.1. The scores for China and India are also

TABLE 9
Environmental Indicators, 2008

	China		India	
	Country Score	Average Score for Country Income Group	Country Score	Average Score for Country Income Group
A				
1. Adequate sanitation	35.4	62.0	21.6	48.2
2. Drinking water	61.0	79.7	76.2	59.6
3. Urban particulates	56.1	83.1	56.6	67.9
4. Indoor air pollution	15.8	67.3	13.9	38.5
5. Industrial CO_2 emissions	49.7	75.5	73.8	85.2
6. Pesticide regulations	59.1	51.5	13.6	41.5
7. Biodiversity and habitat	56.7	53.5	21.2	48.6
8. Fisheries	44.0	74.1	77.2	73.6
9. Environmental burden of disease	94.6	91.5	76.6	78.5
10. Air pollution	44.9	93.0	88.0	89.7
11. Water (effects on ecosystem)	69.6	64.2	65.4	67.4
B				
12. Agriculture	81.5	78.2	55.8	77.7
13. Air pollution (effects on humans)	48.6	78.4	48.2	59.7
14. Water (effects on humans)	47.7	70.9	48.9	53.9
15. Climate change	52.7	71.3	57.9	71.8
C				
16. Aggregate environmental performance index	65.1	76.8	60.3	68.5

Source: Environmental performance estimates prepared by the Yale University Center for Environmental Law and Policy and the Columbia University Center for International Earth Science Information Network.
Note: For China the reference income group is the fifth decile in PPP per capita incomes of the 149 countries; for India it is the seventh decile.
Items under B include some items under A (for example, item 13 includes items 3 and 4).
Item 16 is aggregate of all items.

significantly worse than the average scores in their respective income groups of countries; for China the reference group is the fifth
decile of countries ranked in order of per capita income (PPP) from
the richest to the poorest and for India it is the seventh decile.

Both countries have abysmally low scores for sanitation and indoor air pollution (largely caused by smoke from cooking fires using
traditional fuel, which contributes to high incidence of respiratory
illness, particularly among women); they are also extremely low for
pesticide regulation and biodiversity in India. Both countries' scores
are relatively low for particulate matter in outdoor air in urban areas,
for air and water pollution in general (in terms of their effects on
human health), and for contribution to climate change. Conditions
are much worse in China than in India in industrial CO_2 emissions,
air pollution (in terms of effects on the ecosystem), and fisheries.
The opposite is the case for environmental degradation in agriculture, where China's score is much better than India's.

There is also a rough aggregate estimate of the total value of
"natural capital" per capita for the two countries in the year 2000
that can be found in Hamilton (2006). It was estimated to be $2,223
for China and $1,928 for India. Natural capital is taken here to in-
clude subsoil assets, timber and nontimber forest resources, cropland,
and pastureland. In most countries the value of natural capital far
exceeds that of produced or physical capital. It is the depreciation
of this natural capital that is an important part of environmental
degradation.

In the rest of this chapter we shall discuss some of the issues of
air and water pollution and degradation of environmental resources
in agriculture in the two countries in greater detail. But our focus
on the local commons should not be interpreted as belittling the
impact of global warming on the lives of the poor. So, a few words
on this before we move on. Even though the rich industrial countries are, and have been, largely responsible for this environmental
damage caused by greenhouse gases, in recent years China and India
have been significant contributors, as table 9, item no. 15, indicates.
China is already the largest emitter of carbon dioxide in the world.
The furious pace of construction of Chinese coal-fired power plants

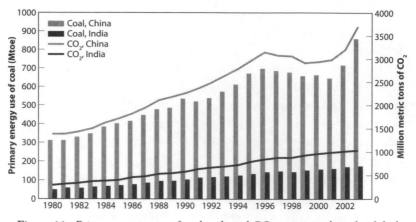

Figure 11. Primary energy use of coal and total CO_2 emissions from fossil-fuel consumption in China and India, 1980–2003. Note: CO_2 = carbon dioxide; Mtoe = million tons of oil equivalent. From Shalizi (2007). Source: International Energy Agency (2005a, b)

(reportedly one new one every week) has caused widespread international concern. India is also dependent on coal as its most important energy source, but to a somewhat smaller extent, and its energy-related emissions are much lower largely because of slower industrialization, urbanization, and rural electrification than in China. Figure 11 plots the time pattern of the use of coal as primary energy source and CO_2 emissions from fossil fuel consumption in the two countries.

Even though Chinese energy efficiency (measured by GDP per unit of energy use in terms of oil equivalent) has been steadily improving over the past few decades, it is still below that of Brazil, India, and the United States. Already acid rain affects nearly one-third of China's land. Global warming, combined with local atmospheric pollution, may lead to a shrinking of the Himalayan glaciers (where many of the river systems of the Indian subcontinent and China originate). This has the potential of an ecological disaster for more than a billion people dependent on these rivers. There are predictions that global warming will considerably change the Indian monsoon pattern, particularly causing lower precipitation in the western half of India, which already contains many dry areas.

Climate change is expected to reduce agricultural output in India more than most other countries, as the temperature increase is expected to be significantly above the global average. The rise in sea level will displace millions of people in the low-lying coastal areas.

II

The more immediately looming problems in both countries are those of air pollution in the cities and water scarcity and toxicity. The World Bank has estimated[1] that the total cost of air and water pollution in China may be as high as 5.8 percent of GDP each year. The cost estimates for air and water pollution available from the Indian Planning Commission are not quite comparable. But the cost of damage to human health from water pollution alone has been estimated at nearly 4 percent of GDP in India. China and India have now eighteen of the world's twenty most polluted cities (most of them in China). For a comparison among world cities in terms of annual levels of particulates, see figure 12. For a comparison of particulate concentrations among cities in northern and southern China and elsewhere in Asia, see figure 13. According to alternative estimates by the World Health Organization, air pollution (both indoor and outdoor) has been the cause of more than a half million premature deaths every year in India, and the number is even higher for China.

In recent years some of the impressive improvements in China from emission controls and change in household fuel away from coal, particularly in urban areas, have been offset by rapid industrialization and the increasing use of personal vehicles for transportation. Although both China and India will remain heavily dependent on coal and petroleum, there are some significant attempts in both countries to develop alternative sources of energy. India already has the world's fourth largest installed wind power capacity. In terms of installation of wind turbines, China has already surpassed the United

---

[1] See World Bank (2007).

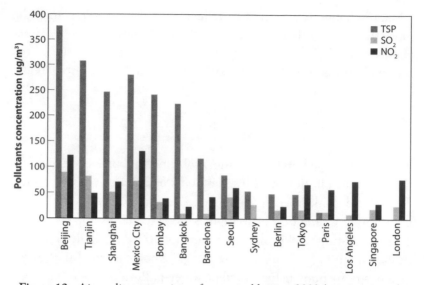

Figure 12. Air quality comparison of some world cities, 2000 (average annual levels of particulates [TSP], SO$_2$, NO$_2$). Note: NO$_2$ = nitrogen dioxide; SO$_2$ = sodium dioxide; TSP = total suspended particulates. Source: Hao and Wang (2005)

States. China's Suntech Company is the third largest manufacturer of solar cells in the world. But given the precarious situation on the energy front, both countries need to make a great deal of further improvement in the sphere of renewable and clean energy.

Pollution of surface and groundwater in both countries is caused by untreated industrial waste, municipal sewage, and fertilizer and pesticide runoffs. In northern China, the water in the 3-H river basins (Hai-Luan, Huai, and Huang) is under severe stress. More than 70 percent of the water in these basins is too polluted for any type of human use. The level of pollution in Indian rivers, though high, has not yet reached that level of widespread toxicity (except some sections of the rivers near big cities, and a much larger part of the water in the Kaveri and Luni river basins may also be under similarly severe stress). The water pollution problem in northern China is compounded by water scarcity. The Huang (Yellow) River, which used to be called "China's sorrow" on account of too much flooding, now is quite dried up in its lower stretches and barely reaches the

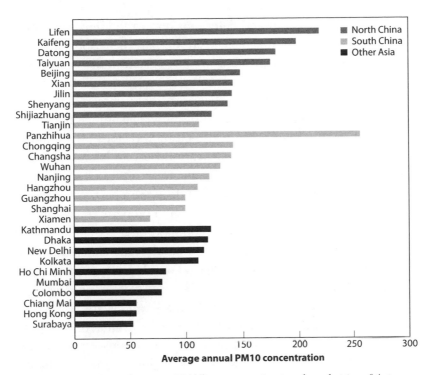

Figure 13. Annual average PM10 concentration in selected cities of Asia.
Note: PM10 = particulate matters of ten microns or less in diameter.
Source: World Bank (2007)

sea. The rivers in southern China are much less dry or polluted. The proposed (and controversial) south-north water transfer project to relieve the thirsty north will be one of the world's largest interbasin water transfer projects. In groundwater, overextraction and water depletion are rampant in northern China and northern and western India. In Punjab, where the Indian green revolution started, about 80 percent of the groundwater blocks are now officially classified as overexploited or critical.

In the green revolution areas, intensive and continuous mono-culture and mining of water has led to soil degradation, waterlogging and salinization, depletion of groundwater aquifers, saltwater intru-sion in the wells in coastal areas, and concentration of nitrates and pesticide residues in drinking water, fisheries, and the food chain.

Severe land degradation and deforestation in the Himalayan foot-hills and in southern China have been the cause of periodic flooding downstream. In western China as well as western India overexploi-tation of grass and forest lands has led to expansion of the deserts. There is also reason to believe that with the disintegration of the village collectives in China, pursuit of individual animal herder in-terests has led to overgrazing in the pastoral regions of the north, aggravating the problem of desertification (just as deforestation ac-celerated with the dismantling of collective control over felling of trees). In general there is also a rapid decline in both countries in the amount of village land that is common property. For example, NSS estimates in India suggest that common-property land declined by more than 7 percent in the Middle- and Trans-Gangetic Plains and by 5 percent in the Eastern Plateau and Hills in just five years, between 1993 and 1998.

In both countries economic growth aspirations are being tem-pered by increased consciousness of their environmental impact. The activist environmental movement is more vigorous in India, but even the Chinese government is now allowing more articula-tion of environmental grievances and requiring more environmen-tal impact statements for projects. There are attempts to link career advancement of local officials with environmental protection goals, but whether this will effectively override their vested interests in local commercial and industrial development remains to be seen.

In the next chapter we discuss the general pattern of vested in-terests and the associated governance issues in both countries from a political-economy viewpoint.

Chapter 10

Looking to the Future:
Through the Lens of Political Economy

Why ponder thus the future to foresee,
And jade thy brain to vain perplexity?
Cast off thy care, leave Allah's plans to Him—
He formed them all without consulting thee.
—Omar Khayyam, *The Rubaiyat*

Winston Churchill once described the qualifications of a politician as "the ability to foretell what is going to happen tomorrow, next week, next month, and next year; and to have the ability afterwards to explain why it didn't happen." Being seriously deficient in both of these abilities and yet frequently confronted with the usual question about the future for both the countries, all I can do is to go over the broad contours of what happened and see if these give us any pointers, and also suggest qualifiers to any straightforward projections of the past into the future. In this chapter, after a telegraphic comparative summary of what has happened to selected aspects of the economy, we shall point to some of the features that may change in near future, and then move on to a broad-brush account of the general structural and political-economy issues that influence the course of economic development as well as the pace of progress in democracy in both countries.

In this context no discussion of China and India can avoid the issues involving the two-way interrelationships between democracy and development. In popular discussion on this topic oversimplifications and clichés abound; in looking to the future, a main purpose of this chapter will be to delve a bit into the complexities that are involved in those interrelationships and associated governance issues. In particular we shall suggest that democracy unleashes both positive and negative forces for development, that there is some tension between the participatory and procedural aspects of democracy in matters of governance as well as economic management, and yet that authoritarianism is neither necessary nor sufficient for development. In India the large proportion of the poor in an assertive electorate has not always succeeded in focusing the attention of the politicians on the sustained implementation of programs to alleviate mass poverty or to deliver basic services such as education and health care. A heterogeneous society, riddled with social and economic inequality and conflict, makes collective action for lasting change difficult to organize and raises populist hindrances to long-term investment (that could cover, for example, India's serious infrastructural deficit) and reform. In a more homogeneous and less conflict-ridden society, China's leadership can be more decisive and purposeful in pursuit of economic reform and long-term strategy, but in the absence of institutionalized checks and balances and of a rule-based system, there is a certain fragility in governance even in an otherwise strong state, and a danger of heavy-handedly overreacting to crisis situations and going off the rails. The decentralized governance structure, which has been a key to rural industrialization in China, has, in the absence of effective mechanisms of democratic accountability, limited the power of central government to rein in local officials from indulging in capitalist excesses in alliance with local commercial interests (resulting in environmental damage, land seizures, violations of consumer product safety standards, and acceleration of economic inequality). In India, local democracy and self-government is still inadequately developed: regular elections at the district level and below are not followed up by effective accountability of government to the local people in most areas (for funding and personnel, local governments are still hopelessly dependent on authorities above, apart from the problems of capture by the local power elite), and the delivery of essential social services and local public goods continues to be dismal. Thus, there are accountability failures in both countries, though their political contexts are different. Sections II–V of this chapter elaborate on the issues summarized in this paragraph.

Both China and India have made remarkable economic progress in the past quarter century, but both have severe structural and institutional problems that will hobble them for many years to come (even after the current problems owing to the global economic downturn have subsided). Between the two countries, China's economic performance has been on balance much better than India's, particularly in rates of economic growth and (rural and labor-intensive) industrialization, in mass poverty reduction, and in the development of physical and social infrastructure. India's fiscal health is much poorer than China's (with implications for leverage to cope with macroeconomic shocks and for social and infrastructure spending). China in recent years[1] has had a small budget surplus (if one counts in the public enterprise profits), whereas India's budget deficit is currently more than 10 percent of GDP (when one includes the off-budget subsidies and loans), one of the highest in the world. Public debt in India is as high as 75 percent of GDP, while China's is about 17 percent.

The financial infrastructure, however, is weaker in China. Even though in both countries the state is dominant in the banking sector, as discussed in chapter 5, the Indian capital market is much more vigorous, with a generally healthier and more active stock market, with less of a burden of bad loans,[2] and with innovative private banks beginning to energize the whole financial services sector. This also reflects the fact that India's domestic private corporate enterprise in industry and services has been more robust and autonomous than China's, and corporate governance usually somewhat more transparent. In China the government, apart from directly dominating much

---

[1] In 2009, with massive stimulus spending the surplus is to turn into a relatively small deficit.

[2] Some of the "nonperforming loans" in government banks in China may be viewed as a disguised budgetary deficit when one compares the large fiscal deficit in India with the low or negative one in China.

of the nonagricultural economy, even now provides private-sector firms very limited access to finance or new markets, and private capital grows only under the all-pervasive shadow of the state and the Communist Party. On the other hand, enterprises in China, even when the control rights are largely held by the state, no longer fit the stereotype of public enterprises and are often highly commercially oriented and in many cases dynamic.

China's future growth will hit the demographic barrier much sooner than India's will. On account of a much faster "demographic transition" in China (in which the better infant mortality record and the one-child policy have played a substantial role), the working-age proportion of the population will peak in the early 2010s, whereas the corresponding peak for India will be reached sometime in the 2030s. Whether India will be able to exploit this demographic window of opportunity will depend on how productively India can employ its relatively young workforce. One should keep in mind that a large part of the population growth will be in the economically less successful and less well-governed large states in northern India. Also, the relative decline in quantity of the workforce in China due to demographic reasons is likely to be counteracted by a rise in quality, with a broader spread of education compared to India. Moreover, with less than a quarter of urban women participating in the labor force (compared to more than 70 percent in urban China), India has a long way to go in the matter of women's contribution to economic growth. Another demographic factor that is likely to cause considerable disruptive social complications[3] in the future (with some economic consequences) is the excessively high male to female ratio in China (as well as in northern and western India).

Although both countries are facing some shortage of skilled labor in a few specific industries and occupations, there is some talk about China's soon running dry in the supply of low-skill labor, which has been a source of high growth there. But, as we saw in chapter 3, China's agricultural sector is still relatively crowded, and the high rate of

[3] For a careful estimate that over the period 1988–2004 the rise in excess males generated by the one-child policy has been responsible for one-seventh of the overall increase in crime in China, see Edlund et al. (2007).

growth of manufacturing wages, which is cited as evidence of labor scarcity, largely reflects the even higher rise in manufacturing labor productivity (and the lingering effects of the official constraints on migration). This is also the reason why, in spite of a higher rate of growth of wages, China's unit labor costs in manufacturing are about the same as India's. In fact, how and where the hundreds of millions of peasants will be absorbed will remain a worrisome question in both countries for the foreseeable future. The problem is, of course, likely to be more acute in India (with India's accretion to the labor force each year being roughly double China's).

The large Chinese pool of household savings, which has funded investment and growth, may decline in importance over time. As China urbanizes (at a distinctly faster rate than India) and the urban-rural income disparity increases, and since the average saving rate for urban households is lower than the rural, the overall household saving rate in China is likely to fall. Also, as the proportion of working-age population falls in China (but rises in India), the household saving rate also will fall in China (but rise in India). In fact, as noted in chapter 5, household saving as a proportion of GDP is already significantly lower in China than in India, whereas enterprise saving and public-sector saving as proportions of GDP are lower in India. If the financial system develops in China, retained earnings of enterprises will decline. Contrary to the popular impression, foreign savings have not been a significant source of the total investment finance (as is evident from China's surplus on the current account of the balance of payments over a large part of the past two decades). It is likely that with increasing competition from other countries and with the looming uncertainties in developed-country markets, Chinese exports as a proportion of GDP will decrease from their hitherto dizzying heights, and whether the slack will be made up by increased domestic consumption to keep up the growth rate largely remains to be seen.

In the long run, the growth performance of an economy depends on technical progress or total factor productivity (TFP) growth. To the extent that TFP in China over the past two decades or more has been driven mainly by the movement from the state to the nonstate sector (where TFP growth has been much higher),[4] its performance will peter out in the very long run as this structural shift exhausts itself over time; but there is still a long way to go, as investment spending is still biased in favor of the state sector and there is a great deal of scope for improved aggregate TFP as the private sector gains in importance. In particular, China's decided policy shift in recent years toward technology promotion and high-tech output composition, major spending on research and development, encouraging large foreign firms' transfer of research activities into the country, investing in high-quality higher education, expansion of biotechnology in agriculture and industry, and so on augur well for sustenance of high TFP growth. Indian policy on all these matters, while being in the same direction, has been on a smaller scale and less sure-footed.[5] In both countries the efficacy of a legal regulatory system in general and a framework for protecting intellectual property rights and incentives for innovation will grow in importance.

As discussed in chapter 9, the severe environmental damage that acts as a drag on effective economic growth and human welfare may in the near future be larger in China than in India. Whether the Chinese central government's energetic countermeasures launched in recent years and determined recent policy of partially reorienting the incentives of local Party cadres from growth to environmental objectives will succeed in having a major impact on the problem remains to be seen.[6] India's countermeasures have yet not reached the scale of China's, but the environmental movement in India is more active as a watchdog. In contrast to India's (relatively) slower depletion of natural capital than China's, India's human capital supply chain is seriously broken (particularly in terms of quantity and quality of primary and secondary school education and of basic health and nutrition), and it will take years to repair it and catch up with

---

[4] For detailed estimates, see Brandt, Hsieh, and Zhu (2008).

[5] According to the July 2008 *McKinsey Quarterly*, average labor productivity in terms of value added in ten high-tech industries was more than thrice in China compared to India in 2006.

[6] The current economic downturn has reportedly slowed down the implementation of some of the proenvironment policies of the government in favor of promotion of industries and jobs.

China and many other developing countries in this respect. We noted
in chapter 7 that, in contrast with inequality of *outcome* (reflected
in income or consumption), inequality of *opportunity*[7] (reflected in
inequality of education, land distribution, and social inequalities) is
much greater in India than in China.

II

Does inequality of opportunity matter for economic growth (apart
from offending one's sense of social justice)? Of course it does, if one
keeps in mind that barriers faced by the poor in land and capital
markets and in skill acquisition and in coping with risks sharply reduce a society's potential for productive investment, innovation,
and human resource development. They often block the creation of
socially more efficient property rights (for example, in land tenure)
and investment in high-risk but high-return innovative projects. Inequality that keeps the workforce largely uneducated and unhealthy
cannot be beneficial for private business, even aside from the law and
order problems that inequality-generated conflicts may bring about.
Moreover, institutional structures and opportunities for cooperative
problem-solving are often forgone by societies that are highly polar-
ized. Equity and efficiency thus often go together, contrary to the
presumption of much of mainstream economics.

In India, however, considerations of equity have often been used
as an excuse for all kinds of regulatory excesses. In the name of helping the poor and small farms and firms, many restrictions on private
initiative and on capacity expansion and many programs of government subsidies and handouts have been launched and prolonged.
Economic reformers have rightly pointed out that most often these
policies and programs did not help the poor (and there certainly exist more cost-effective ways of helping them), while distorting the

[7] Those who emphasize equality of opportunity are sensitive to the issue of individual
responsibility; two people with the same opportunity may justifiably end up with different
outcomes or incomes simply because one works harder, is more ambitious, or the like (this is
salient, for example, in the egalitarian philosophy of Ronald Dworkin).

economic incentives for enterprise and investment and protecting the rental havens of politically well-connected oligarchies. In other words, they helped the cause of neither efficiency nor equity.

At the same time, in a country that in terms of inequality of opportunity and intergenerational mobility may be one of the worst in the world, as noted in different parts of this book, Indian reformers have to be extremely sensitive to (the public perception of) equity issues if they hope to move the cause of economic reform, which has in general been rather halting and hesitant over the past two decades. Cheerleaders of reform among corporate tycoons and financial columnists are often unaware how unpopular reform is, rightly or wrongly, among the general public in India. In the National Election Survey 2004, more than two-thirds of about twenty-three thousand sample respondents (who had any opinion on the subject) said that the reforms benefit only the rich or none at all.[8] Politicians are, of course, too savvy not to notice this. Any of the ruling parties over the past two decades that supported reforms played them down during election time. A party that initiates some reforms is quick to oppose them when out of power.

Economic reform, as it aims to bring about more competition, inevitably causes job disruptions and displacements that raise the level of anxiety among workers, particularly in a country of very little general social protection. Trade unions of the right as well as left parties in India are opposed to privatization and to relaxation of the job security regulations in labor laws. The Gandhians as well as the leftists were vocal against the lifting of the policy of reservation for small-scale industries (and other policies of positive discrimination in favor of small enterprises). In the National Election Survey mentioned earlier, respondents were asked about reduction in the size

---

[8] See Suri (2004). This was also confirmed in a smaller January 2007 survey by the same team from the Center for Study of Developing Societies (CSDS). Of course reformers have also done a poor job of explaining reforms to the common people. If it were to be made clear to them, for example, that electricity reform, which may involve a higher electricity price, also implies a higher capacity for the public utility to provide less erratic power supply, or that deregulation means loosening the grip of corrupt inspectors on small enterprises, some of the opposition might decline. In fact, the January 2007 CSDS survey found that 63 percent of the respondents were prepared to pay higher rates for electricity if it were regularly supplied.

of government; among the poor, the low-caste, and the indigenous respondents who had an opinion, the majority was opposed to such reduction. The newly emergent, hitherto subordinate, social groups, often represented by primarily caste-based or regional parties, as they capture state power and reserved jobs, are clearly not too keen on giving up the loaves and fishes of office or reducing the role of the public sector (where at the lower echelons the salaries are about three times what one would get in the private sector with similar qualifications).[9]

What financial columnists are quick to describe as antireform populism is partly a product of the manifold inequalities and conflicts of Indian society. The severe educational inequality, for example, makes it harder for many to absorb the shocks in the industrial labor market, since education and training could provide some means of flexibility in adapting to market changes. In China the disruptions and hardships of restructuring under a more intense process of global integration were rendered somewhat tolerable in the 1980s and 1990s by the fact that China has had some kind of a minimum rural safety net, largely made possible by an egalitarian distribution of land-cultivation rights in 1978–1979. In most parts of India, for the poor there is no similar rural safety net. So the resistance to the competitive process that market reform entails is that much stiffer in India. This is in line with a worldwide phenomenon: resistance to globalization is generally stronger in countries where social safety nets (particularly unemployment benefits and portable health insurance) are weaker (compare the Scandinavian countries and the United States in this respect).

In general, social heterogeneity and economic inequality make the social and political environment in India quite conflict-ridden, and it is difficult in this environment to build consensus and organize collective action toward long-term reform and cooperative

---

[9] The ambiguous attitude of poor people toward the state is evocatively expressed by Luce (2007): "To the poor the state is both an enemy and a friend. It tantalizes them with a ladder that promises to lift them out of poverty but it habitually kicks them in the teeth when they turn to it for help. It inspires both fear and promise. To India's poor the state is like an abusive father whom you can never abandon. It is through you that his sins are likely to live on."

problem-solving efforts.[10] When groups don't trust one another in the sharing of costs and benefits of long-term reform, there is the inevitable tendency to opt instead for the "bird-in-hand" short-run subsidies and government handouts, which pile up as an enormous fiscal burden. Very few politicians dare oppose the continuing serious underpricing of water and electricity (along with fertilizers, domestic fuels such as kerosene and liquified petroleum gas and gasoline, railway passenger fare, tuition in higher education institutions, etc.), the overmanning of the public payroll, and a long-standing refusal to tax the better-off farmers.

This is a general problem of collective action in a country where even the elite is highly fragmented. In terms of social and economic divisions, the Indian elite may be more fragmented than the elite in most other countries, not just China, reflecting the fact that India has one of the world's most heterogeneous societies (in terms of language, religion, caste, and ethnic divisions). The resultant collective-action problem makes it more difficult for the divided elite groups to agree on a goal, and even when they agree on a goal, it is difficult for them to coordinate their actions to achieve that goal. This becomes a particularly acute political-economic problem in the matter of long-term public investment in infrastructure (power, roads, transportation, telecommunications, ports, irrigation, etc.). As discussed in chapter 4, infrastructure is widely regarded as the crucial bottleneck for Indian economic growth, and the Indian elite would largely benefit from any improvement in infrastructure. Yet substantial public investment in infrastructure, which takes a relatively long time to fructify, may require significant short-run sacrifices; in the current situation of large fiscal deficits, this means the elite (and the so-called middle classes) giving up government subsidies or benefits of underpriced public goods and services, or salary or perks in government jobs, or allowing for major increases in taxes and user charges. But coordinating on short-run sacrifices or curbing particularistic demands on the public fisc (it has been estimated

[10] This is in line with a large theoretical and empirical literature on the relationship between inequality and collective action—see, for example, Baland and Platteau (2006) and Bardhan (2005).

that about two-thirds of all government subsidies go to the relatively rich) for the sake of long-term elite goals has been very difficult to achieve in India.[11]

Of course, in the past two decades the old rent-sharing equilibrium (among business firms, the salariat, and rich farmers) has changed somewhat and tilted in favor of capitalist business. The hegemony of the latter is reflected in the more general acceptance of probusiness policies and reform in trade and industrial policy without a great deal of opposition in policy circles. Although infrastructure remains a bottleneck, there is a more general consensus on the other major public good—macroeconomic stability—as a precondition for economic growth. Inflation control has remained high on the public agenda, but there has been less agreement on a whole range of other reforms, particularly relating to the factor markets (labor, land, electricity, etc.) and on fiscal subsidies and rent-sharing with the newly emerging social groups. Collective-action problems abound in most of these cases, where at the micropolicy implementation level the conflicting interests of large numbers of people are involved and transmission of information to the central decision-makers is weak.

There are two kinds of collective-action problems. One relates to sharing the costs of bringing about change (the "free-rider problem"); the other relates to sharing the benefits (the "bargaining problem"). Over the years, both of these collective-action problems have become more severe. As more and more hitherto subordinate social groups have become politically important, particularly at the state level (in a welcome expansion of political equality and democracy in India), the sources of demands on the polity have become more diverse. In the first two decades after Independence, the massive countrywide organization of the Congress Party used to coordinate transactional negotiations among different groups and leaders in various parts of the country. That once-mighty organization has fallen into disarray. The proliferation of small and regional parties and their increasing importance for the survival of coalition governments

---

[11] This was the central point of Bardhan (1984) in discussing the collective-action problem that hinders public investment in India.

at the center have often meant that catering to particularistic demands overrides coordination for the long haul.

When the interest groups are socially and economically fragmented, pulling in different directions with none dominating the whole show, state policies get buffeted, and any steps toward economic reform are likely to be halting and hesitant. But at the same time, such fragmentation may also give the state somewhat more autonomy, in the sense that it does not have to march to the tune of one dominant interest group,[12] and an astute political leadership can play off one group against another and get its way to some extent, and even earn its own rent in the form of special power and privileges. In such a context, the state leadership can retain some potency as an organizational actor in goal formulation, agenda-setting, and policy execution, even when it acts within the broad constraints of interest-group politics. Such autonomy[13] of a government may also allow it to take advantage of the malleability and fragmentation of interest groups to diffuse some resistance to reform. It is in this context that one can see the point made by Jenkins (2000) that the Indian political system has clever, if sometimes clandestine, ways of introducing many kinds of reforms—what he calls "reform by stealth,"[14] that accommodations arranged through informal political networks mediate conflicts between winners and losers, and that particular reform measures generate a chain reaction of demand for more reform from within.

Although liberalization has meant a significant reduction in the discretionary powers of the central bureaucracy, particularly in trade policy and industrial regulations, the state governments still retain a great deal of leverage over the industrial sector at the ground level through their control of land, water, electricity, and labor and envi-

[12] Yadav and Palshikar (2009) have even suggested that in recent years, as the complexities of competitive politics at the multiplicity of state levels rise, the aggregating coalition governments at the center can have some policy autonomy that can operate somewhat independently of the particularities of political contestation in individual states.

[13] This is related to the old Marxist literature on the "relative autonomy of the state."

[14] "Reform by stealth" usually does not work when it affects large groups. It cannot be substantial and purposive enough to break, for example, the basic political logjam in the macroeconomy caused by the staggering fiscal burden of subsidies to different interest groups.

ronmental regulations. Different states apply these regulations with different degrees of alacrity, and the differing political attitudes to creating a hospitable investment climate for private capital often reflect political conflicts within the state. There is a growing body of public opinion that the state should mainly be a facilitator in the industrial and service economy and reorient its role away from public ownership and control of business enterprises and toward more focus on health, education, and other basic social services for the poor, and that even when the state is to be the major funding agency for some of these services, it does not necessarily mean that the actual provision of the services has to be bureaucratically managed, instead of being contracted out to the private sector or some form of private-public partnership. But, in spite of some progress, the political implementation of this view in large parts of India has been slow and fitful.

Market reforms in India are also resisted by environmentalists and those concerned with the rights of urban squatters and of the indigenous and other marginalized people. In general, the people who eke out their fragile living in the overwhelmingly large informal sector, particularly in the periphery of the urban economy, use their political/electoral power of numbers to negotiate with the state some forms of tenuous protection against the onslaught of the market and legality.[15] Markets, and capitalist development in general, have become identified with uprooting the livelihoods of the little people and despoliation of the environment. The record of resettlement and rehabilitation of people displaced by roads or dams or mining projects is dismal in India, and recent history of such projects is replete with arbitrary land requisitions, defrauding by contractors, and reneging on promises to these poor people. This is the context of widespread opposition to land requisition for commercial purposes in India. The Indian government's attempt to replicate the Chinese-style Special Economic Zones has hit this formidable roadblock in some, though not all, states.

[15] Chatterjee (2004) emphasizes the importance of the contingent, and often paralegal, negotiations between the state and what he calls "political society" of the poor in Indian cities.

If inequality and social heterogeneity have played a role in the resistance to reform in India, in recent years mounting inequality has been a source of major concern for the reformers in China as well (as much as for the "new left" in the Chinese intelligentsia). Some have already linked this with the tens of thousands of incidents of unrest in different parts of the country, reported even in Chinese official police records. One should not, however, exaggerate the extent of inequality-induced discontent in the rural and remote areas of China. Data from a 2004 national representative survey in China,[16] carried out by Martin Whyte, a Harvard sociologist, and his team show that the presumed disadvantaged people in the rural or remote areas do not seem to be particularly upset by the rising inequality.

A major component of Chinese inequality is the rural-urban disparity. Yet the rural respondents in the survey report more gains from the reform era, more satisfaction from their current living standards, and less "distrust" of the system than their urban counterparts; two-thirds of them say that life is "better" or "much better" now compared to five years back. This is not unexpected in this fast-growing economy when even in rural areas the average per capita household income increased at an annual rate of nearly 5 percent in 1991–2004. Even across expenditure groups, the bottom quintile in China experienced a significant 3.4 percent growth rate in mean per capita expenditure between 1993 and 2004 (the corresponding figure for the bottom quintile group in India is only 0.85 percent). Also, the Chinese rural people may perceive more opportunities opening up with the relaxation of restrictions on mobility from villages and improvement in roads and transportation.

The great majority of both urban and rural respondents (more urban than rural), however, consider the degree of inequality in the country "too large" (but not so much in their own neighborhood). The more urban and educated people display more distrust of the system. There is rural unrest, but, paradoxically, the potential for unrest may be more problematic in the booming urban areas, par-

---

[16] This survey, called the National Survey of Perception of Distributive Justice in China, involved a sample of nearly 3,300 respondents from the entire national adult population. Some of the results reported in the text are from Wang (2007).

ticularly as the real estate bubble breaks, and if the global slowdown ripples devastatingly through the excess-capacity industries and financially shaky public banks. With a more Internet-connected and vocal middle class, and the rise in unemployment (and wage and severance payment arrears) in the current downturn on top of a history of massive worker layoffs in the recent past and a large underclass of migrants, urban unrest may be more difficult to contain. As it is, a kind of guerilla warfare between cyber-censors and those who are intent on beating the system ("tunneling under the great firewall") constantly goes on over the Internet, and in times of a serious crisis in the future it may be difficult for the government to keep a lid on the spread of bad news.[17]

What inflames the passions of farmers is land requisitions (apart from toxic pollution of their land and water), rather than inequality as such. It is reported that by 2006 more than sixty million farmers in China had lost their land to the demands of commercialization and development, without adequate compensation; in spite of the sound and fury, the Indian land requisitions so far have been nowhere near that scale. Land sales to developers used to provide "extrabudgetary revenues" to local governments in China, and also kickbacks pocketed by local Party officials. As noted in chapter 3, the recent land laws of the central government have tried to stop this; whether they will succeed will depend on their control of the process of decentralized development and of the link between local development and the cadre reward system. But in most of the scattered incidents of rural unrest, the central government has so far succeeded in keeping public wrath focused on the local officials, and containing it and not allowing it to snowball. (In the 2004 national survey mentioned earlier, 27 percent of rural respondents say that they have been treated unfairly by local officials.) Some opinion polls suggest that central leadership remains popular even as local officials are not.

---

[17] Of course, the Internet sometimes helps the government by allowing citizens to let off steam, or in deflecting public anger toward (and putting pressure on) local officials. On the other hand, some growing "rights activism" in defense of property rights and the environment—the *weiquan* movement—over the Internet can be a source of worry for the government.

When China started the reform process, in the early years cautiously orchestrated change in the household responsibility system with individual cultivation rights, dual-track pricing (with both planned and market allocations coexisting), competition with new entry and management incentives but no privatization, and rural industrialization under decentralization with TVEs mostly represented reform with very few losers[18] (except for recipients of some social services) and minimum social and economic disruption. In later years, as market allocations, commercialization, and corporate restructuring of firms prevailed, millions of workers were laid off from state enterprises, and as the "iron rice bowl" of social protection for employees was to a large extent broken, there were many losers. But by that time the fast-growing economy was able to absorb and compensate many of the losers, though the benefits were unequally spread. In recent years, forcible land requisition and pollution have created more losers. Yet opposition to reform is scattered and sporadic. Even in the laggard rural and remote areas, roads, telecommunications, and outmigration have opened new opportunities. The government also assuaged grievances in recent years by announcing policies to abolish agricultural taxes and fees and to introduce free education (up to ninth grade) and some rudimentary social insurance, and of attempting to lessen the discriminatory treatment that many migrants face in cities.

Indian economic reform as such may not yet have produced as many losers. Most of the reforms so far relate to trade and industrial policy and the fiscal and the financial sectors, which have led to a restructuring of the corporate sector (still a relatively small contributor to total employment), but without much of a change in the labor laws that are supposed to ensure job security of those already employed in the small formal sector or in the policy of (implicit and explicit) fiscal subsidies for many goods and services. Not all the disruptions caused by commercial development can be attributed to market reforms. To the extent that reforms have directly caused the exit of some inefficient firms and some diversion away from subsi-

---

[18] See Lau, Qian, and Roland (2001).

dized "priority lending" of the banking sector to small farmers and small and medium enterprises, some people may have lost out. But the reforms of the kind that have a larger potential for disrupting the livelihoods of a substantial number of people—such as labor reform, or price reform in water and electricity, or large-scale privatization and streamlining of the public-sector enterprises, or the entry of large retail chains in marketing—have so far been successfully resisted. The major issue on which a large number of farmers and tribals are offering stiff resistance is that of land requisition in different parts of the country for industrial, commercial, and large irrigation and mining projects. The main resistance is from people who distrust official promises of compensation and rehabilitation, are wary of environmental damage to their familiar habitat, and whose low level of education and skills make them unlikely to be direct beneficiaries from the new, more productive jobs to be created.

III

Resistance and protests are, of course, more organized and strident and politically consequential under Indian democracy than under Chinese authoritarianism. This brings us to the general issue of democracy and development, which no discussion of China and India can avoid. But much of the standard discussion of the subject is full of simplistic clichés or high-minded platitudes. China's dramatic success has revived a hoary myth that particularly in the initial stages of economic development authoritarianism delivers much more than democracy. This is also supported by the memory of impressive economic performance of other East Asian authoritarian regimes (such as those in South Korea and Taiwan in the recent past). The lingering hope of democrats had been that as the middle class prospers in these regimes, they then demand—and in the latter two cases eventually got—movement toward political democracy.

But the relationship between authoritarianism or democracy and development is not so simple. Authoritarianism is neither necessary nor sufficient for economic development. That it is not necessary is illustrated not only by today's industrial democracies but also by scattered recent cases of successful development: Costa Rica, Botswana, and now India. That it is not sufficient is amply evident from disastrous authoritarian regimes in Africa and elsewhere.

Even if we were not to value democracy for its own sake (or regard it as an integral part of development by definition), and were to view it in a purely instrumental way, it is worth reiterating the several advantages of democracy from the point of view of development. First, democracies are better able to avoid catastrophic mistakes (such as China's Great Leap Forward and the ensuing great famine that killed nearly thirty million people, or the massive mayhem of the Cultural Revolution), and they have greater healing powers after difficult times. In general, democracy makes for a better capacity for managing conflicts, which in the long run makes possible a more stable political environment for development. India's democratic pluralism has provided the means of containing many (though not all) social conflicts, a capacity that I am not sure China's homogenizing, monolithic state has so far acquired. Faced with a public crisis or political shock, the Chinese leadership, which is otherwise so pragmatic, has a tendency to overreact, suppress information, and act heavy-handedly. (One example of a ruthless heavy-handed state: some accounts by human rights organizations suggest that, while both countries have capital punishment, China executes more people in one week than India has done in total in the more than sixty years since Independence; capital punishment data are actually rather shaky in both countries, but the qualitative point remains starkly valid.)

Some degree of tolerance for diversity and dissent has historically been the safety valve for India's extremely heterogeneous society. Indian history is replete with cases of polyglot profusion, dissenting sects rebelling against Brahminical high culture, and a multiplicity of syncretic folk traditions. For many centuries, on the contrary, Chinese high culture, language, and political and historiographical tradition have not given much scope to pluralism and diversity, and a centralizing, authoritarian Communist Party has carried on this tradition. Jenner (1992), in his provocative book analyzing the link between the "history of tyranny" and the "tyranny of history" in China, describes one of the most basic tenets of Chinese civilization as "that uniformity is inherently desirable, that conflict is bad, that there should be only one empire, one culture, one script . . . , one tradition," and that "what is local and different is treated [by the high culture] as deviant." Nurtured in this tradition, there is a certain preoccupation in China (not just in the Party) with order and stability and the importance of avoiding *da luan* (great turmoil) and a quickness to brand dissenting movements and local autonomy efforts as seditious, and this often leads to unnecessarily heavy-handed repression.

In recent years, China has diffused and contained many conflicts by localizing them. In a more positive and constructive direction, the policy of decentralized development and regional autonomy has encouraged local initiative and incentives. But in order to keep these local initiatives within some moderate bounds and to make them serve national goals through tournament-like competition in regional economic performance, centralized control was maintained through the channels of promotion and the system of rewarding local officials from above. But centralized control is, of course, not always benign, even though the Party leadership has in recent years curbed some of its arbitrary practices and shown some sensitivity to popular grievances. But as long as checks and balances on the top leadership are not fully institutionalized, the danger of going off the rails in response to unexpected events and exaggeration of dissent always remains.

Democracies in general experience more intense pressure to share the benefits of development among the people and to reduce the human costs of dislocation, thus making development more sustainable. They also provide more scope for popular movements against capitalist excesses and industrial fallout such as environmental degradation. In addition, there are more political opportunities to mitigate social inequalities (especially acute in India) that act as barriers to social and economic mobility and to the full development of individual potential.

Finally, democratic open societies provide a better environment for nurturing the development of information and related technologies, a matter of some importance in the current knowledge-driven global economy. Intensive cyber-censorship in China may seriously limit some forms of future innovation in this area. Generally censorship (and, more often, anticipatory self-censorship) inhibits people's imaginativeness and inventiveness. State control of information also sometimes makes for delay in official recognition, and thus handling, of a developing crisis. From the SARS outbreak to the recent tainted milk scandal, there are many examples of this. Weeks before the latter scandal broke, journalists were encouraged to suppress bad news in view of the imminent Olympics, which was being stage-managed as China's moment of international glory. Journalists who were fully aware of the tainted milk case avoided writing about it "in order to be harmonious," as one editor said later (see report in the *New York Times*, September 27, 2008). Meanwhile, nearly three hundred thousand children fell sick, and considerable damage was done to the reputation of Chinese products.

All that said, India's experience suggests that democracy can also hinder development in a number of ways not usually considered by democracy enthusiasts. Competitive populism—short-run pandering and handouts to win elections—may hurt long-run investment, particularly in physical infrastructure, which is the key bottleneck for Indian development. Such political arrangements make it difficult, for example, to charge user fees for roads, electricity, and irrigation, discouraging investment in these areas, unlike the situation in China, where infrastructure companies charge more commercial rates. Competitive populism also makes it difficult to carry out policy experimentation of the kind the Chinese have excelled at throughout their reform process. For example, it is harder to cut losses and retreat from a failed project in India, which, with its inevitable job losses and bailout pressures, has electoral consequences that discourage leaders from carrying out policy experimentation in the first place.

Electoral politics, particularly in a divided society with a weak civic culture of pursuit of general welfare, can also give rise to clientelism, in which there is an implicit quid pro quo between voter support and official disbursement of benefits specific to some individuals or a particular social group, at the expense of broader-based benefits from public goods. This also generates more pressure for recurring short-run benefits and subsidies for which the politician can claim privately identifiable and immediate credit, at the expense of long-gestation public investment projects.

In Indian democracy, the legislative process is often relegated to a second order of importance, giving short shrift to the deliberative process in the legislature that John Stuart Mill and other theorists of democracy valued so much. The legislature has become an arena for slogan-mongering, shouting matches, and a generous display of the theater of the absurd. Important bills are often passed without much discussion, sometimes in less than an hour. On many controversial issues, the opposing parties do not try to resolve them in legislative deliberations but quite literally take to the streets for this purpose. They (including the ruling party) concentrate on organizing mass rallies and counterrallies and a show of strength in popular mobilization, often taking pride in how their followers have paralyzed the daily life of a city. By and large, India is less a legislative or deliberative democracy than one of popular mobilization. This means that issues that could be resolved through deliberative give-and-take get trapped in rhetorical intransigence and the strident divisiveness of street theater, and thus decision deadlocks are frequent, which has immense political and economic costs. This is over and above the general case that democracy's slow decision-making processes can be costly in a world of fast-changing markets and technology.

Besides, when democracy takes mainly the form of popular mobilization in a country where the general education level is low, civic associations relatively weak, and public debates relatively uninformed, the opposition can get away with being irresponsible (short-sighted and often opposing the government on policies they themselves supported when in power). It also gives political opportunists a lot of leeway to divide the electorate on ethnic, regional, or religious lines, which gives rise to easy ways of political "fishing in troubled waters." Fomenting sectarian fear and anxiety is often a successful political mobilization device.

The hopes of democrats relying on the middle classes in authoritarian regimes have not always borne fruit. Latin American and

Southern European history has been replete with episodes of the middle class hailing a supreme caudillo. The police state in China shows no signs of loosening its grip soon, despite spectacular progress in the opening of the economy. Although there has been some relaxation in controls over individual expression of thought or lifestyle, and some open middle-class grumbling over pollution and forcible requisition of property, the state never fails to clamp down on political activities that have even a remote chance of appearing to challenge the central authority's monopoly of power. Most people in the Chinese middle class are complicit in this in the name of preserving social stability or "harmony," as long as opportunities for moneymaking and wallowing in nationalist pride keep on thriving. A kind of preening nationalism has replaced socialism as the social glue in China, with the state leadership occasionally trying to stoke and then modulate collective passions about what the West or Japan did in the past to China during the "century of humiliation" (sometimes fomented by frenzy on the Internet) and to turn any external criticism into a slur on national self-respect.

Indian urban middle classes also have a prickly nationalism, but more than harking back to the two centuries of direct colonial subjugation, it occasionally turns instead to majoritarian atavism to serve as unifier in the context of unmanageable social and cultural diversity in the society and works itself up questioning the national loyalty of domestic minority groups (in a context in which the violent partition of the country at Independence remains a festering wound). The urban upper and middle classes in many parts of India are impatient about climbing the global ranks of the big powers and often regard the numerically large poor outside their gated communities, with their all too visible squalor and messy democratic politics, as a hindrance and a liability.[19]

---

[19] Aravind Adiga captures this in his novel *The White Tiger* when the rich master in a conversation with his wife in front of his servant/driver refers to the latter in the following way: "He can read and write, but he doesn't get what he's read. He's half-baked. The country is full of people like him. . . . And we entrust our glorious parliamentary democracy . . . to characters like these. That's the whole tragedy of this country."

IV

Democracy has clearly brought about a kind of social revolution in India. It has spread out to the remote reaches of this far-flung country in ever-widening circles of political awareness and self-assertion of hitherto socially subordinate groups. These groups have increased faith in the efficacy of the political system and they vigorously participate in larger numbers in the electoral process. In the National Election Survey, the percentage of respondents who answered yes to the question "Do you think your vote has an effect on how things are run in this country?" increased between 1971 and 1996 from 45.7 percent to 57.6 percent for "backward caste" groups (designated as OBC in India), from 42.2 percent to 60.3 percent for the lowest castes (designated as scheduled castes), 49.9 percent to 60.3 percent for Muslims, and from 48.4 percent to 58.7 percent for all groups taken together. In a 2004 survey[20] it was found that 56 percent of OBC people, 48 percent of the lowest castes, and 55 percent of Muslims as well as of the general population were satisfied ("somewhat" or "very") with the way democracy works in the country.

But the great puzzle of Indian democracy is why the poor people, who are so assertive when election time comes, often seem not to punish politicians who are ineffective in resolving the endemic problems of poverty, disease, and illiteracy. It is possible that endemic poverty is widely regarded among common people as a complex phenomenon with multiple causes, and they ascribe only limited responsibility to the government in this matter. The measures of government performance are in any case rather noisy, particularly so in a world of illiteracy and low levels of civic organization and formal communication on public issues. A perceived slight in the speech of a political leader felt by a particular ethnic group will usually cause much more of an uproar than if the same leader's policy neglect keeps thousands of children severely malnourished in the same ethnic group. The same issue of group dignity comes up in the case of reservation of public-sector jobs for backward groups, which

[20] See State of Democracy in South Asia (2008).

fervently catches their public imagination, even though objectively the overwhelming majority of the people in these groups have no chance of ever landing those jobs, as they and their children largely drop out of school by the fifth grade. Even when these public job quotas mainly help the tiny elite in backward groups, as a symbol and a possible object of aspiration for their children they ostensibly serve a valuable function in attempts at group upliftment.

Particularly in northern India there seems to be a preoccupation with symbolic victories among the emerging lower-caste political groups; as Hasan (2000) points out with reference to BSP, a politically successful party of the socially oppressed in Uttar Pradesh, these groups seem less concerned about changing the economic-structural constraints under which most people in their community live and toil. Maybe this is just a matter of time. These social and political changes have come to northern India rather late; in southern India, where such changes took place several decades earlier, it may not be a coincidence that there has been much more effective performance in the matter of public expenditures on pro-poor projects such as health, education, housing, and drinking water. This reflects the fact that in southern India there has been a long history of social movement against the exclusion of lower castes from the public sphere, against their educational deprivation, and so on in a more sustained and broader-based way than in northern India. One may also note that the upper-caste opposition to social transformation is somewhat stronger in northern India, as demographically upper castes constitute in general a larger percentage of the population than has been the case in most parts of southern India. So new political victories of lower castes in northern India get celebrated in the form of defiant symbols of social redemption and recognition aimed at solidifying their as yet tentative victories rather than in committed attempts at changing the economic structure of deprivation.

Although the electorate does not seem to penalize politicians for their endemic poverty, they are less forgiving when there is a sharp and concentrated deterioration in their economic condition. Sen (1983) has commented on the political sensitivity of democracies to the threat of famine, but to me the more commonplace example for this in India is the electorate's high degree of inflation sensitivity. It is a common presumption that an annual inflation rate at the double-digit level, if it continues for some time, will be politically intolerable in India, and politicians universally support a conservative monetary and sometimes even fiscal policy to avoid this danger. The poor tend to make the government directly responsible for inflation and expect it to stop it in its tracks even at the expense of cutting budgetary programs on infrastructure or social services that would have helped the poor in the long run—as they say, contra Keynes, *in the short run* "we are all dead," when the country is poor and incomes are largely unindexed in the face of high inflation.

The Indian electorate has often been regarded as reflexively anti-incumbent,[21] particularly in contrast with the electorate in the United States. This may have something to do with the widespread dissatisfaction of the electorate with the delivery of social services and public goods (along with the related problems of corruption). Some evidence—see Banerjee and Somanathan (2007)—does suggest that some low-caste groups (which were better mobilized than others) improved their access to the benefits of expansion of public goods in the 1970s and 1980s; this was particularly in contrast with other disadvantaged groups such as the indigenous people and Muslims. Since the poor usually get mobilized on caste and ethnic lines, the modalities of such mobilization are often multidimensional, and poverty alleviation is only one of the many issues that get articulated in the public domain. Also, the process of such ethnic mobilization is often easy to hijack for the elite of these groups, who channel a lion's share of the benefits to themselves. The intended poor beneficiaries are often unorganized and uninformed about their entitlements, and they also lack the ability to evaluate the quality of the particular education or health-care service provided.

Besides, at any given moment in India an election somewhere is not far off (as national, state, or municipal or village council elections are staggered) and, as in election times everywhere in the world,

---

[21] In very recent elections this has not always been the case, and there have been some states where incumbent governments with a reputation for better performance have been reelected—as evidenced in the parliamentary elections of 2009.

short-term calculations dominate. Populist quick-fix policies rather than sustainable improvements in structural conditions become the order of the day, and since in India's extremely fractious society it is usually the case that no disadvantaged group by itself is numerically predominant, exigencies of electoral alliances with other groups (some of them not so disadvantaged) dilute the need for attending to the poorest. Since the better-off people (including better-off sections of disadvantaged groups) increasingly turn to private sources of supply of public services (primary and secondary education, health care, irrigation, drinking water, child nutrition), the political support structure for public access to these services or improvement in their quality is rather weak or getting eroded in many parts of the country. There are also differential degrees of public vigilance over (or effectiveness of) different types of antipoverty programs. As mentioned earlier, political clientelism prevails, under which delivery of private and short-run benefits (in the form of temporary employment projects, subsidies, loan waivers, etc.) takes priority over delivery of public services and long-term investment in infrastructural facilities (roads, public health and sanitation, watershed development, etc.).

The problem of poor delivery of social services is not just a problem of lack of public vigilance or demand; it is, of course, a serious governance problem from the supply side as well (such as inadequate supply of school buildings or health clinics with appropriate facilities within manageable distance; rampant absenteeism by teachers, doctors, and nurses; etc). This is where governance mechanisms of local accountability become salient.

Decentralization of governance in the sense of devolution of power to elected local governments was constitutionally adopted in India around the same time as economic reforms. It was supposed to increase accountability of the service bureaucracy as well as generate resources to address felt needs at the local level. But this particular governance reform as yet remains largely ineffective, except in three or four states, and in this sense local democracy is still rather weak in India. In most cases, the local government officials are primarily involved in selecting beneficiaries of programs designed and funded from above. A large number of local governments simply do not have adequate funds, or the appropriate delegated functions, or competent functionaries to carry out locally initiated autonomous projects that could make a significant difference in the lives of the poor; and there is considerable misappropriation of funds and delivery of services to nontarget groups, sometimes giving decentralization a bad name. Yet there have been some localized success stories.

In China decentralization has been successful, as pointed out earlier, in providing incentives (and discipline) for rural industrialization.[22] But decentralization has increased regional inequalities, with richer coastal regions having better ability to fund social services. The inequality of initial conditions undermines the efficacy even of antipoverty programs. As Ravallion (2007) shows, under *Di Bao*, the large urban antipoverty program that aims to assure a minimum income through means-tested transfers, poor municipalities systematically understate their poverty problem and apply inappropriate eligibility conditions in beneficiary selection, since otherwise they would have to commit commensurate local resources to the program, thereby reducing the program's ability to reach poor areas.

In spite of the fiscal recentralization of mid-1990s and a great deal of central transfers to local areas, there is a widespread rural budget crisis in China. The system is still sufficiently fiscally decentralized, with large numbers of unfunded mandates and social obligations for the local governments, that while the better-off regions can afford superior public services,[23] the lagging regions have to live with large cuts in community services or to pass along much of the costs to be borne by service users (some of them very poor). The tensions of fiscal federalism are increasing in India too. The

[22] In India, local business development has not usually been on the agenda of local governments. There are some exceptions in Kerala. Consider, for instance, the Manjeri municipality in the relatively backward district of Malappuram in northern Kerala. In collaboration with some social groups and bankers, the municipal authorities succeeded in converting it into a booming hosiery manufacturing center, after developing the necessary skills and finance at the local level.

[23] This is also partly because the wealthier coastal provinces managed to extract from Beijing a tax rebate transfer as part of the 1994 fiscal recentralization deal.

better-performing state governments are now openly protesting large redistributive transfers to laggard states ordained by the Finance Commission. In the Indian democratic system, however, some of these laggard populous states (such as Uttar Pradesh or Bihar) send a very large number of members to the Parliament, and the (shaky) coalition governments at the center can usually ill afford to alienate them.

V

There are interesting contrasts in the style and content of governance in China and India. In China there is more decisive policy initiative and execution than in India. This is not all due to an authoritarian setup. In general, collective-action problems in goal formulation and policy enforcement are, as indicated earlier, less severe in China than in the conflict-ridden and extremely heterogeneous society of India, where any major controversial decision is preceded by endless discussion, loud agitation, breast-beating street antics, and sometimes even fist fights, property damage, and running battles with police; ultimately what gets carried out after considerable delay is a much-fought-over and imperfect compromise. But for the same reason, executive authority in India, though weak, is more legitimate. The same disorderly processes of fractious pluralistic democracy that make decisiveness on the part of the leadership difficult, make it more legitimate in the eyes of the people. The Chinese leadership, on the other hand, has to derive popular legitimacy from ensuring rapid economic growth, and now after several years of high growth, also partly from advancing toward "harmonious" goals (i.e., environment-friendly growth with some rudimentary social protection and effective political order), apart from protecting people from the immediate effects of the global economic slump. Ethnicity-based dignity politics, group upliftment, and other sectarian issues that crowd the political agenda in India are less of an encumbrance on the pursuit of those goals in China; on the other hand, the global slump is less regime-threatening in India.

In recent years, the political leadership in China has also been more technocratic and professional[24] than in India, which helps in informed, purposive decision-making and in maintaining something like a corporate culture even in the Party bureaucracy. Promotions in the administrative services are more performance-based (rather than seniority-based) in China than in India. "Transfers and postings" of officials is a major preoccupation (and sometimes a source of illicit income) of Indian politicians, particularly at the state level. Rotation and temporary sojourns of Indian bureaucrats in a given job inhibits on-the-job learning of their increasingly complex tasks. Regulatory effectiveness in commercial transactions is also better in China than in India,[25] even though *guanxi* and corruption continue to contaminate the process. Nepotism in state appointments may have, however, gone further in China than in India: it is reported that many of the senior positions in some of the state-dominated sectors in China are filled by the children and other relatives of high-ranking Party officials. Some Chinese economists have warned about the dangers of crony capitalism.

Corruption is pervasive in both countries. But corruption in China is qualitatively different from that in India in at least three ways: (1) in China the lines of authority are more well-defined and streamlined, whereas there is multiple veto power of different authorities (part of the checks and balances system) on a given decision in India[26]—and as a result, even after paying bribes, one is never sure if the job will get done; (2) since official rewards and promotions in China are more directly linked to local economic performance than in India, the officials involved do not usually lose sight of the overall

---

[24] Even the Communist Party membership composition in China has changed substantially in the past quarter century. In 1978, two-thirds of the members were workers and peasants. By 2005, their share fell to 29 percent; 23 percent of members are now professionals and 30 percent college students. This may have been part of the post-Tiananmen adaptation by the Party to coopt professionals and students.

[25] The World Bank surveys in connection with *Doing Business 2008* suggest that both in registering property and in enforcing contracts, the Indian system involves more procedures, delays, and higher costs than the Chinese system does.

[26] An apocryphal story has it that one high official in New Delhi told a friend, "If you want me to move a file faster, I am not sure I can help you; but if you want me to stop a file, I can do it immediately."

performance record, even as they line their own pockets; and (3) as elections become more expensive, politicians in India have to be on the lookout to collect serious money to an extent not necessary in China. But at the same time there are more institutionalized efforts in India to check the sources of corruption: the Right to Information Act, for example, which recently came into existence as a result of an energetic public activist movement in India is an important step in that direction.

The social revolution that democracy has brought about, which we noted earlier, has also had some impact on the nature of governance in India. The diminishing hold of elite control and the welcome expansion of democracy to reach the lower rungs of the social hierarchy have been associated with a loosening of the earlier administrative protocols and a steady erosion of the institutional insulation of the decision-making process in public administration and economic management. This has affected not just the ability to credibly commit to long-term decisions, but the whole fabric of governance itself. It is now common practice, for example, for a low-caste chief minister in a state to proceed, immediately upon assuming office, to transfer away top civil servants belonging to upper castes and replace them with pliant bureaucrats from his/her own caste. Some of the new social groups coming to power are even nonchalant in suggesting that all these years upper classes and castes have looted the state, so now it is their turn. If in the process they trample on some individual rights or some procedural aspects of democratic administration, the institutions that are supposed to kick in to restrain them are relatively weak. Highly corrupt politicians are regularly reelected by their particular ethnic or local constituencies (which they nurse assiduously even while fleecing the rest of the system). Personal extravagance at state expense by particular ethnic leaders is often a source of community pride for historically disadvantaged groups.

This is part of a fundamental tension between the *participatory* and *procedural* aspects of democracy in India: the unfolding of the logic of populist democracy has itself become a threat to democratic governance. Kaviraj (1995) has described this as a strange Tocquevillian paradox: "Democratic government functioned smoothly in the early years after 1947 precisely because it was not taking place in a democratic society; as democratic society has slowly emerged, with the spread of a real sense of political equality, it has made the functioning of democratic government more difficult." Some people are not too worried by this, and they regard it as part of the initial necessary turmoil of democratic movement forward and group self-assertion. The writer V. S. Naipaul (1997), who is fascinated by the "million mutinies" in contemporary India, says: "When people start moving, the first loyalty, the first identity, is always a rather small one. . . . When the oppressed have the power to assert themselves, they will behave badly. It will need a couple of generations of security and knowledge of institutions and the knowledge that you can trust institutions—it will take at least a couple of generations before people in that situation begin to behave well."

One wishes one could share this optimistic belief in democratic teleology. The breakdowns in democratic governance and economic management structures are not easy to repair and there are irreversibilities in institutional decay. Besides, in India's multilayered social structure, by the time one self-aware group settles down and learns to play by the institutional rules, other newly assertive groups will come up and defy those rules, often in the name of group equity.

The participatory aspects of democracy and the all-consuming emphasis on electoral mobilization often of whole groups (described by journalists as "vote banks") lead the system to look away from the politicians' and their followers' rampant procedural violations, and this generates a "culture of impunity" that the Indian political system will have to grapple with for quite some time to come. Of course, ultimately the checks and balances of the ramshackle but still vibrant legal system kick in to curb undue excesses, in a way that is rather rare in China. The independent judiciary (exerting itself in selection of judges and building up case law and through public interest litigation), the Election Commission, the commissions on human rights and on minorities, and a few of the regulatory bodies still function with some degree of insulation from the political interference and hold up due process against great odds.

This institutional insulation is much weaker in China, and the "culture of impunity" of top Party officials is more prevalent. But there has been discernible progress in the legal system: as disputes become more complex, political interference, though still substantial, is declining, particularly in matters of commercial law. There is greater transparency than before in corporate governance in state companies, particularly those listed on overseas stock exchanges. The media and the NGO movement as watchdogs are, of course, more active in India. But corporate ownership of media is a problem for independent investigations in both countries, though in different ways. There is occasional official clamping down on corruption in China (including even summary execution as punishment), but cynical people often describe this as mostly targeted at political enemies or at best small fry, exempting big fish or cronies of the dominant faction leaders.

The Party has also tentatively started to experimentally introduce some form of intraparty democracy at the lower levels, with multiple candidates for positions.[27] It is ironic that Indian democracy, which in the beginning decades allowed for a great deal of intraparty democracy, now has largely deviated from this tradition. In most major national parties the local leaders are often nominated from above. Young and ambitious local politicians, finding their path of upward mobility blocked within the larger parties, often are inclined to go out and form their own party, and acquire quite a bit of leverage in the coalition politics of India. This is one source of the increasing political fragmentation in India that makes purposive governance more difficult.

We discussed in chapter 2 the important role that decentralization of power combined with central control over personnel and promotion play in Chinese governance. In recent years the central government has recentralized the public finances (as it was facing fiscal erosion by the mid-1990s) and taken over the final authority over personnel and loan decisions of local banks (to check the increase

[27] For an account of this and other fledgling electoral experiments at the local level, see Thornton (2008).

of "nonperforming loans" in which local officials had indulged). But the local government even at the county level has still a great deal of power (much more than in India) in privatizing state companies, in regulatory approvals and patronage distribution, in appointing local oversight committees against financial and other irregularities, in appointment of (and fixing salaries of) judges and public prosecutors, and so on. It is difficult for the central government to control local officials and wean them away from the cozy rental havens they have built in collusion with local business and commercial interests. The central government in its pursuit of the goals of reducing inequality, stopping land seizures, containing environmental damage, and preventing the frequent regulatory scandals (relating to food and other consumer product safety) face at least the covert opposition of local officials.[28] Even when the local official is not venal, in an atmosphere of information control his usual inclination is to suppress bad news, as it may adversely affect his chances of promotion or his reputation. Pei (2008) quotes the lament of a former vice minister of education that "politics cannot get out of Zhongnanhai" (the central government headquarters in Beijing) and comments that this captures the dilemma of a one-party state that is powerless to force its will on its own agents. The legal and political checks on local officials that the central leadership occasionally introduces are periodically undermined by the same leadership, as it is wary of the opportunities for legal and political activism that those checks may encourage to unmanageably leap across local boundaries.

Yet over more than a quarter century now the Chinese central leadership has shown a remarkable adaptability to changing circumstances and capacity to mobilize new support coalitions to protect its political power.[29] Keeping the main focus on economic growth and national glory as the source of its political legitimacy, it moved away from its earlier constituent groups among peasants and workers in allowing urban-rural disparity to grow and presiding over massive

---

[28] In recent years in some areas the government has increased administrative control and fiscal oversight over villages and townships to an extent that leaves few incentives for initiative by local officials, a situation that is closer to that familiar in India.

[29] For a perceptive account, see Naughton (2008).

layoffs of workers; it accommodated the erstwhile "red-hat capitalists" in symbiotic relationship with state officials, and gradually coopted the new private entrepreneurs and professionals (including much of the intelligentsia); through its control of bank lending and regulatory approval of investment it has skillfully balanced regional and factional interests. It is now trying to move some state resources away from the government-business groups of coastal China (for example, those connected with what used to be called the "Shanghai coalition"), and has publicly shown a great deal of empathy for hitherto excluded groups in remote rural areas and urban migrants, while still being supportive of markets and general noninterference with thriving private enterprises. By streamlining rules of succession and establishing clear procedures about term and age limits for leaders, it has restructured the rules of authoritarian hierarchy to increase career predictability and general elite support.

But it is still far from establishing a comprehensive rule-based system and institutionalizing a credible set of checks and balances. It has installed a far more decisive and purposive governance structure than India has, but its weaker institutional checks (such as lack of an independent judiciary or other regulatory authority or countervailing social organizations or independent bottom-up institutions) and low capacity for conflict management make it more brittle in the face of a crisis than the messy-looking system in India, despite all its flaws. As the economy becomes more complex and social relations become more convoluted and intense, the absence of transparent and accountable processes and the attempts by a "control-freak" leadership to enforce conformity and lockstep discipline will generate acute tension and informational inefficiency. Several alternative political scenarios for the future in China have been depicted by political speculators, none more plausible than the others; some (wistfully) predict the eventual outbreak of Taiwanese- or Korean-style democracy but only on a large scale, starting with the big cities; others predict that even if China manages a soft landing into some form of quasi democracy, it will be of the corrupt oligarchic kind under a predominant party like the one that prevailed in Mexico under PRI for many decades.

Although the Indian system has lot more institutionalized outlets for letting off steam, it also has more ethnic and religious tensions and centrifugal forces to grapple with. Its appalling governance structure for delivery of social services, its anomic inability to carry out collective action or to overcome populist hindrances to long-term investment to address the infrastructural deficit that is reaching crisis proportions, its overpoliticized administration and decision-making processes, its clogged courts and corrupt police and patronage politics frequently making a mockery of the rule of law for common people will all continue to hobble the process of economic growth and alleviation of India's still massive poverty. Yet the differential capacity and governance performance among different states (better in some southern or western Indian states) may generate over time a bit of healthy competition in investment climate and poverty alleviation performance to set examples for the democratic participants in all states to demand, overshadowing the salience of ethnicity or religion in politics. The slowly emerging importance of development governance and a slight improvement in political coherence in recent electoral results are hopeful straws in the wind.

Although both China and India have done much better in the past quarter century than they did in the past two hundred years in the matter of economic growth, and although both polities have shown a remarkable degree of resilience in their own ways, one should not underestimate their structural weaknesses and the social and political uncertainties that cloud the horizon for these two countries. It will indeed be a sign of "vain perplexity" to pronounce judgment on how and when these clouds will clear.

REFERENCES

Anderson, K. 2009. *Distortions to Agricultural Incentive: A Global Perspective*. New York: Palgrave Macmillan.

Appleton, S., J. Knight, L. Song, and Q. Xia. 2002. "Labor Retrenchment in China: Determinants and Consequences." *China Economic Review* 13 (2–3): 252–275.

Asian Development Bank. 2007. *Key Indicators 2007: Inequality in Asia*. Manila: Asian Development Bank.

Bai, C.-E., and Y. Qian. 2008. "Infrastructure Development in China" Manuscript, Tsinghua University, Beijing.

Balakrishnan, P., and M. S. Babu. 2003. "Growth and Distribution in the Indian Industry in the Nineties." *Economic and Political Weekly* 38 (38): 3997–4005.

Baland, J.-M., and J.-P. Platteau. 2006. "Collective Action on the Commons: The Role of Inequality." In *Inequality, Cooperation, and Environmental Sustainability*, ed. J.-M. Baland, P. Bardhan, and S. Bowles. Princeton, NJ: Princeton University Press.

Banerjee, A., S. Cole, and E. Duflo. 2004. "Banking Reform in India." *India Policy Forum* 1:277 323.

Banerjee, A. and R. Somanathan. 2007. "The Political Economy of Public Goods: Some Evidence from India." *Journal of Development Economics* 82 (2): 287–314.

Bardhan, P. 1984. *The Political Economy of Development in India*. New Delhi: Oxford University Press. Expanded edition, 1998.

———. 2005. *Scarcity, Conflicts, and Cooperation*. Cambridge, MA: MIT Press.

Benjamin, D., L. Brandt, J. Giles, and S. Wang. 2008. "Income Inequality during China's Economic Transition." In *China's Great Economic Transformation*, ed. L. Brandt and T. G. Rawski. New York: Cambridge University Press.

Borooah, V. K., B. Gustaffson, and L. Shi. 2006. "China and India: Income Inequality and Poverty North and South of the Himalayas." *Journal of Asian Economics* 17:797–817.

Bosworth, B., and S. M. Collins. 2007. "Accounting for Growth: Comparing China and India." *Journal of Economic Perspectives* 22 (1): 45–66.

Bosworth, B., S. M. Collins, and A. Virmani. 2007. "Sources of Growth in the Indian Economy." *India Policy Forum 2006/07* 3:1–69.

Brandt, L., C. Hsieh, and X. Zhu. 2008. "Growth and Structural Transformation in China." In *China's Great Economic Transformation*, ed. L. Brandt and T. G. Rawski. New York: Cambridge University Press.

Brandt, L., T. G. Rawski, and J. Sutton. 2008. "China's Industrial Development." In *China's Great Economic Transformation*, ed. L. Brandt and T. G. Rawski. New York: Cambridge University Press.

Branstetter, L., and N. Lardy. 2008. "China's Embrace of Globalization." In *China's Great Economic Transformation*, ed. L. Brandt and T. G. Rawski. New York: Cambridge University Press.

Cai, F., A. Park, and Y. Zhao. 2008. "The Chinese Labor Market in the Reform Era." In *China's Great Economic Transformation*, ed. L. Brandt and T. G. Rawski. New York: Cambridge University Press.

Cai, X., and M. W. Rosegrant. 2007. "Future Prospects for Water and Food in China and India: A Comparative Assessment." In *The Dragon and the Elephant: Agricultural and Rural Reforms in China and India*, ed. A. Gulati and S. Fan. Baltimore: Johns Hopkins University Press.

Chand, R., and P. Kumar. 2004. "Determinants of Capital Formation and Agriculture Growth: Some New Explorations." *Economic and Political Weekly* 39 (52): 5611–5616.

Chatterjee, P. 2004. *The Politics of the Governed: Reflections on Popular Politics in Most of the World*. New York: Columbia University Press.

Chaudhuri, S., and M. Ravallion. 2006. "Partially Awakened Giants: Uneven Growth in China and India." In *Dancing with Giants: China, India, and the Global Economy*, ed. L. A. Winters and S. Yusuf. Washington, DC, and Singapore: World Bank and Institute of Policy Studies.

Chen, S., and M. Ravallion. 2008. "The Developing World Is Poorer than We Thought, but No Less Successful in the Fight against Poverty." Policy Research Working Paper no. 4073, World Bank, Washington, DC.

Dasgupta, M. 2005. "Public Health in India: An Overview." World Bank Policy Research Working Paper no. 3787, World Bank, Washington, DC.

Datt, G., and M. Ravallion. 2002. "Has India's Post-Reform Economic Growth Left the Poor Behind?" *Journal of Economic Perspectives* 16 (3): 89–108.

Deaton, A., and V. Kozel, eds. 2005. *The Great Indian Poverty Debate*. New Delhi: Macmillan.

Deshpande, L. K. 2004. *Liberalization and Labor: Labor Flexibility in Indian Manufacturing*. New Delhi: Institute of Human Development.

Ding, N., and Y. Wang. 2008. "The Household Income Mobility in China and Its Decomposition." *China Economic Review* 19 (3): 373–380.

Dutta Roy, S. 2004. "Employment Dynamics in Indian Industry: Adjustment Lags and the Impact of Job Security Regulations." *Journal of Development Economics* 73 (1): 233–256.

Edlund, L., H. Li, J. Yi, and J. Zhang. 2007. "Sex Ratios and Crime: Evidence from China's One-Child Policy." IZA Discussion Paper no. 3214, Institute for the Study of Labor, Bonn.

Evans, P. 1995. *Embedded Autonomy: States and Industrial Transformation*. Princeton, NJ: Princeton University Press.

Fan, C. S., and X. Wei. 2006. "The Law of One Price: Evidence from the Transitional Economy of China." *Review of Economics and Statistics* 88 (4): 682–697.

Fan, G., D. H. Perkins, and L. Sabin. 1997. "People's Republic of China: Economic Performance and Prospects." *Asian Development Review* 15 (2): 43–85.

Fan, S., L. Zhang, and X. Zhang. 2004. "Reforms, Investment, and Poverty in Rural China." *Economic Development and Cultural Change* 52 (2): 395–422.

Friedman, T. L. 2005. *The World Is Flat: A Brief History of the Twenty-first Century*. New York: Farrar, Straus & Giroux.

Giles, J., A. Park, and F. Cai. 2006. "Reemployment of Dislocated Workers in Urban China: The Role of Information and Incentives." *Journal of Comparative Economics* 34 (3): 582–607.

Giles, J., A. Park, and J. Zhang. 2005. "What Is China's True Unemployment Rate?" *China Economic Review* 16 (2): 149–170.

Goldberg, P. K., A. Khandelwal, N. Pavcnik, and P. Topalova. 2008. "Imported Intermediate Inputs and Domestic Product Growth: Evidence from India." NBER Working Paper no. 14416, National Bureau of Economic Research, Cambridge, MA.

Groves, T., Y. Hong, J. McMillan, and B. Naughton. 1995. "China's Evolving Managerial Labor Market." *Journal of Political Economy* 103 (5): 873–892.

Guo, H., R. W. Jolly, and J. Zhu. 2007. "Contract Farming in China: Perspectives of Farm Households and Agri-business Firms." *Comparative Economic Studies* 49:285–312.

Guo, Y., and C. Xu. 2006. "Subnational Government and Corporate Governance in China: Evidence from a Nationwide Survey." Typescript, Beijing University.

Gupta, P., R. Hasan, and U. Kumar. 2008. "What Constrains Indian Manufacturing?" Working Paper no. 211, Indian Council for Research on International Economic Relations, New Delhi.

———. 2009. "Big Reforms but Small Payoffs: Explaining the Weak Record of Growth and Employment in Indian Manufacturing." MPRA Paper no. 13496, University Library of Munich, downloadable at http://mpra.ub.uni-muenchen .de/13496/.

Haggard, S., and Y. Huang. 2008. "The Political Economy of Private-Sector Development in China." In *China's Great Economic Transformation*, ed. L. Brandt and T. G. Rawski. New York: Cambridge University Press.

Hamilton, K., ed. 2006. *Where Is the Wealth of Nations? Measuring Capital for the 21st Century*. Washington, DC: World Bank.

Hammer, J., Y. Aiyar, and S. Samji. 2007. "Understanding Government Failure in Public Health Services." *Economic and Political Weekly* 42 (40): 4049–4057.

Hao, J., and L. Wang. 2005. "Improving Air Quality in China: Beijing Case Study." *Journal of the Air and Waste Management Association* 55:1298–1305.

Hasan, Z. 2000. "Representation and Redistribution: The New Lower-Caste Politics of North India." In *Transforming India: Social and Political Dynamics of Democracy*, ed. F. R. Frankel et al. New Delhi: Oxford University Press.

Heston, A. 2008. "What Can Be Learned about the Economies of China and India from Purchasing Power Comparisons?" Typescript, University of Pennsylvania.

Hsieh, C.-T., and P. J. Klenow. 2007. "Misallocation and Manufacturing TFP in China and India." NBER Working Paper no. W13290, National Bureau of Economic Research, Cambridge, MA.

Huang, Y. 2006. "Assessing Financing Constraints for Domestic Private Firms in China and India: Evidence from the WBES Survey." Special issue. *Indian Journal of Economics and Business* (September 2006): 69–92.

———. 2008. *Capitalism with Chinese Characteristics*. New York: Cambridge University Press.

International Energy Agency. 2005a. CO_2 *Emissions from Fuel Combustions*. Paris: Organisation for Economic Co-operation and Development.

———. 2005b. *Energy Balances of Non-OECD Member Countries, Extended Balances*. Paris: Organisation for Economic Co-operation and Development.

Jenkins, R. S. 2000. *Democratic Politics and Economic Reform in India*. Cambridge: Cambridge University Press.

Jenner, W.J.F. 1992. *The Tyranny of History: The Roots of China's Crisis*. London: Penguin Press.

Kaviraj, S. 1995. "Democracy and Development in India." In *Democracy and Development*, ed. A. K. Bagchi. New York: St. Martin's Press.

Khan, A. R. 2004. "Growth, Inequality, and Poverty in China." Issues in Employment and Poverty Discussion Paper no. 15, International Labor Office, Geneva.

Khor, N., and J. Pencavel. 2006. "Income Mobility of Individuals in China and the United States." *Economics of Transition* 14 (3): 417–458.

Kuijs, L. 2005. "Investment and Saving in China." Policy Research Working Paper no. 3633, World Bank, Washington, DC.

———. 2006. "How Will China's Saving-Investment Balance Evolve?" Policy Research Working Paper no. 3958, World Bank, Washington, DC.

Kumar, S., A. Heath, and O. Heath. 2002. "Changing Patterns of Social Mobility: Some Trends over Time." *Economic and Political Weekly* 37 (40): 4091–4096.

Lau, L. J., Y. Qian, and G. Roland. 2001. "Reform without Losers: An Interpretation of China's Dual-Track Approach to Transition." *Journal of Political Economy* 108 (1): 120–143.

Li, D. 1998. "Changing Incentives of the Chinese Bureaucracy." *American Economic Review* 88 (2): 393–397.

Li, H., L. Meng, Q. Wang, and L.-A. Zhou. 2008. "Political Connections, Financing and Firm Performance: Evidence from Chinese Private Firms." *Journal of Development Economics* 87 (2): 283–299.

Li, H., and L.-A. Zhou. 2005. "Political Turnover and Economic Performance: The Incentive Role of Personnel Control in China." *Journal of Public Economics* 89 (9–10): 1743–1762.

Lin, J. Y. 1992. "Rural Reforms and Agricultural Growth in China." *American Economic Review* 82 (1): 34–51.

Lin, T., J. Zhuang, D. Yarcia, and F. Lin. 2008. "Income Inequality in the People's Republic of China and Its Decomposition: 1990–2004." *Asian Development Review* 25 (1–2): 119–136.

Lipton, M., and M. Ravallion. 1995. "Poverty and Policy." In *Handbook of Development Economics*, vol. 3B, ed. J. Behrman and T. N. Srinivasan. Amsterdam: Elsevier.

Luce, E. 2007. *In Spite of the Gods: The Strange Rise of Modern India*. New York: Doubleday.

Maddison, A. 2007. *Chinese Economic Performance in the Long Run*. Paris: OECD Development Center.

Maddison, A., and H. Wu. 2008. "Measuring China's Economic Performance." *World Economy* 9 (2): 13–44.

Mazumdar, D., and S. Sarkar. 2008. *Globalization, Labor Markets, and Inequality in India*. New York: Routledge.

McNally, C. A. 2007. "China's Capitalist Transition: The Making of a New Variety of Capitalism." In *Capitalisms Compared*, ed. L. Mjoset and T. H. Clausen. Oxford: Elsevier.

Mohan, R. 2008. "Growth Record of the Indian Economy, 1950–2008: A Story of Sustained Savings and Investment." *Economic and Political Weekly* 43 (19): 61–71.

Montalvo, J. G., and M. Ravallion. Forthcoming. "The Pattern of Growth and Poverty Reduction in China." *Journal of Comparative Economics.*

Nagaraj, R. 2008. "India's Recent Economic Growth: A Closer Look." *Economic and Political Weekly* 43 (15): 55–61.

Naipaul, V. S. 1997. Interview in *India Today* 22:36–39.

National Statistical Commission. 2001. Report, Ministry of Statistics and Program Implementation, Government of India, New Delhi.

Naughton, B. 2008. "A Political Economy of China's Economic Transition." In *China's Great Economic Transformation*, ed. L. Brandt and T. G. Rawski. New York: Cambridge University Press.

Organisation for Economic Co-operation and Development. 2005. *OECD Economic Surveys: China*. Paris: Organisation for Economic Co-operation and Development.

———. 2007. *OECD Economic Surveys: India*. Paris: Organisation for Economic Co-operation and Development.

Patel, U., and S. Bhattacharya. 2008. "Infrastructure in India: The Economics of Transition from Public to Private Provision." Typescript, Reliance Industries Ltd., Mumbai.

Pei, M. 2008. "How China Is Ruled." *American Interest* 3 (4): 44–51.

Perkins, D. H., and T. G. Rawski. 2008. "Forecasting China's Economic Growth to 2025." In *China's Great Economic Transformation*, ed. L. Brandt and T. G. Rawski. New York: Cambridge University Press.

Pinglé, V. 1999. *Rethinking the Developmental State: India's Industry in Comparative Perspective*. New York: St. Martin's Press.

Poncet, S. 2005. "A Fragmented China: Measure and Determinants of China's Domestic Market Disintegration." *Review of International Economics* 13 (3): 409–430.

Prestowitz, C. 2005. *Three Billion New Capitalists: The Great Shift of Wealth and Power to the East*. New York: Basic Books.

Purfield, C. 2006. "Mind the Gap—Is Economic Growth in India Leaving Some States Behind?" IMF Working Paper no.06/103, International Monetary Fund, Washington, DC.

Ravallion, M. 2007. "Geographic Inequity in a Decentralized Anti-Poverty Program: A Case Study for China." World Bank Research Policy Working Paper no. 4303, World Bank, Washington, DC.

Ravallion, M., and S. Chen. 2007. "China's (Uneven) Progress against Poverty." *Journal of Development Economics* 82 (1): 1–42.

Reidel, J., J. Jin, and J. Gao. 2007. *How China Grows: Investment, Finance, and Reform*. Princeton, NJ: Princeton University Press.

Ren, X., and L. Weinstein. 2008. "The Shanghai Effect: Political Devolution and Mega-Project Development in China and India." Center for Advanced Study of India, http://casi.ssc.upenn.edu/node/127.

Reserve Bank of India. 2008. *Handbook of Statistics on the Indian Economy, 2007–08*. Mumbai: Reserve Bank of India.

Rozelle, S., L. Brandt, G. Li, and J. Huang. 2002. "Land Rights in China: Facts, Fictions and Issues." *China Journal* 47:67–97.

Sen, A. K. 1983. "Development: Which Way Now?" *Economic Journal* 93:745–762.

Shalizi, Z. 2007. "Energy and Emissions: Local and Global Effects of the Giants' Rise." In *Dancing with Giants: China, India, and the Global Economy*, ed. L. A. Winters and S. Yusuf. Washington, DC, and Singapore: World Bank and Institute of Policy Studies.

Shi, L., Z. Wei, and S. Jing. 2005. "Inequality of Wealth Distribution of Chinese People: An Empirical Analysis of Its Cause." FED Working Paper no. 65, China Center of Economic Research, Peking University, Beijing.

Sicular, T., X. Yue, B. Gustaffson, and Shi Li. 2007. "The Urban-Rural Gap and Income Inequality in China." *Review of Income and Wealth* 53 (1): 93–126.

Sinha, A. 2005. *The Regional Roots of Development Politics in India*. Bloomington: Indiana University Press.

Srinivasan, T. N. 2008. "Some Aspects of Price Indices, Inflation Rates, and the Services Sector in National Income Statistics." In *Footprints of Development and Change*, ed. N. Jayaram and R. S. Deshpande. New Delhi: Academic Foundation.

Srinivasan, T. N., and P. K. Bardhan. 1974. *Poverty and Income Distribution in India*. Calcutta: Statistical Publishing Society.

State of Democracy in South Asia. 2008. *State of Democracy in South Asia: A Report*. New Delhi: Oxford University Press.

Suri, K. C. 2004. "Democracy, Economic Reforms and Election Results in India." *Economic and Political Weekly* 39 (51): 5404–5411.

Thornton, J. 2008. "Long Time Coming: The Prospects of Democracy in China." *Foreign Affairs* 87 (1): 2–22.

Topalova, P. 2007. "Trade Liberalization, Poverty, and Inequality: Evidence from Indian Districts." In *Globalization and Poverty*, ed. A. Harrison. Chicago: University of Chicago Press.

———. 2008. "India: Is the Rising Tide Lifting All Boats?" IMF Working Paper no.08/54, International Monetary Fund, Washington, DC.

Tsai, K. S. 2007. *Capitalism without Democracy: Private Sector in Contemporary China*. Ithaca, NY: Cornell University Press.

Vashisht, P., et al. 2006. "Report on Electricity Subsidies to Agriculture in Andhra Pradesh and Punjab." Typescript, National Council of Applied Economic Research, New Delhi.

Virmani, A., and S. Mittal. 2006. "Domestic Market Integration." ICRIER Working Paper no. 183, Indian Council for Research on International Economic Relations, New Delhi.

Wang, F. 2007. "Boundaries of Inequality: Perceptions of Distributive Justice among Urbanities, Migrants, and Peasants." Center for the Study of Democracy Paper 07-09, University of California, Irvine.

Wang, Z., and S.-J. Wei. 2008. "What Accounts for the Rising Sophistication of China's Exports?" NBER Working Paper no. 13771, National Bureau of Economic Research, Cambridge, MA.

Winters, L. A., and S. Yusuf, eds. 2007. *Dancing with Giants: China, India, and the Global Economy*. Washington, DC, and Singapore: World Bank and Institute of Policy Studies.

World Bank. 2007. *Report on Costs of Pollution: Economic Estimates of Physical Damages*. Washington, DC: World Bank.

Wu, H., P. Rao, and B. Lee. 2008. "A Comparison of Real Output and Productivity between Indian and Chinese Manufacturing Industries Using Industry-of-Origin PPP Approach." *ICP Bulletin* 5 (2): 23–31.

Xu, C. 2008. "The Institutional Foundations of China's Reforms and Development." Posted at www.sef.hku.hk/~cgxu/working%20paper/Xu_Regional%20Decentralization_1-21-09.pdf.

Yadav, Y., and S. Palshikar. 2009. "Principal State-Level Contests and Derivative National Choices: Electoral Trends in 2004–09." *Economic and Political Weekly* 44 (6): 55–62.

Yip, W., and A. Mahal. 2008. "Health Care Systems of China and India: Performance and Future Challenges." *Health Affairs* 27 (4): 921–932.

Young, A. 2000. "The Razor's Edge: Distortions and Incremental Reform in the People's Republic of China." *Quarterly Journal of Economics* 115 (4): 1091–1136.

Zhang, J., Y. Zhao, A. Park, and X. Song. 2005. "Economic Returns to Schooling in Urban China, 1988 to 2001." *Journal of Comparative Economics* 33 (4): 730–752.

INDEX